Traveler Steve

Sofia
Travel Guide 2025

Unveiling Hidden Gems, Savoring Local Cuisine, Exploring Historic Sites, and Insider Tips for a Memorable Journey

Traveler Steves

Copyright

Copyright © 2024 [Traveler Steves].

All rights reserved.

No part of this publication may be reproduced, distributed, or transmitted in any form or by any means, including photocopying, recording, or other electronic or mechanical methods, without the prior written permission of the publisher, except in the case of brief quotations embodied in critical reviews and certain other noncommercial uses permitted by copyright law.

For permission requests, write to the publisher at the address below:

[phdphilcharles@gmail.com]

INTRODUCTION   7

Why Sofia in 2025?   10

Fun facts and trivia   13

Chapter One   19

GETTING TO SOFIA   19

Direct flights and major airlines   19

Visa Requirements and Entry Procedures   24

Transportation Options from the Airport   28

Chapter Two   35

INSIDER TIPS FOR A MEMORABLE JOURNEY   35

The best times to visit   35

Local etiquette and customs   43

Money-Saving Tips   50

Apps and Resources for Travelers   55

Chapter Three   65

WHERE TO STAY IN SOFIA — 65

Top hotels and accommodations — 65

Budget-Friendly Hostels — 90

Unique Stays: Boutique Hotels and Airbnb's — 113

Chapter Four — 139

EXPLORING SOFIA'S NEIGHBORHOODS — 139

Vitosha Boulevard is the heart of the city. — 139

Boyana: Suburban Charm and Historic Monasteries — 146

Lozenets: Upscale Living and Trendy Cafes — 152

Chapter Five — 159

HISTORIC SITES AND CULTURAL ATTRACTIONS — 159

Alexander Nevsky Cathedral — 159

The National Palace of Culture — 165

Sofia History Museum — 172

Ancient Serdica Archaeological Complex — 178

Sofia Zoo — 185

Chapter Six   193

HIDDEN GEMS   193

The Bells Monument   193

Vrana Palace   199

Borisova Gradina Park   205

Mineral Baths and Spas   212

Boyana Church   219

Chapter Seven   227

SAVORING LOCAL CUISINE   227

Traditional Bulgarian dishes to try   227

The Best Restaurants for Authentic Food   239

Markets and street food   244

Vegetarian and vegan options   251

Chapter Eight   259

NIGHTLIFE AND ENTERTAINMENT   259

The Best Bars and Clubs   259

Venues for live music	264
Theatrical Performances and Cultural Events	270
Local festivals and traditions	274
Seasonal festivals and celebrations	276

Chapter Nine   283

SHOPPING IN SOFIA   283

Trendy Boutiques and Fashion Stores	283
Local Crafts and Souvenirs	288
Flea Markets and Antique Shops	293

Chapter Ten   301

OUTDOOR ACTIVITIES AND DAY TRIPS   301

Hiking in Vitosha Mountain	301
Guided Tours	305
Day Trips to Rila Monastery and Plovdiv	307
A day trip to Plovdiv	314
Cycling Routes and Parks	320
Exploring Borisova Gradina	324

Winter sports and ski resorts	329
Chapter Eleven	**343**
## PRACTICAL INFORMATION	**343**
Public Transportation Guide	343
Safety Tips and Emergency Contacts	348
Traveling with Your Pet: A Guide to Pet-Friendly	351
## CONCLUSION	**359**
Recap of Key Highlights	359
Explore Beyond the Guide	360
Final Thoughts	361

INTRODUCTION

LONG-AWAITED to Sofia, a city where history meets modernity, where every street tells a story, and there you're assured to find something new around every corner. Whether you're a first-time visitor or a seasoned tourist, Sofia has a way of making everyone feel like they belong.

Sofia city

Consider this: cobblestone streets taking you to ancient ruins, cozy cafes inviting you for a break, and lively markets bustling with life. Doesn't that sound like the kind of place you'd love to explore? Sofia is a city that seamlessly mixes the old with the new.

As you stroll through its charming streets, you'll encounter an eclectic mix of architectural styles, from Roman ruins and medieval churches to elegant Austro-Hungarian buildings and modern glass structures. This unique fusion creates a captivating backdrop that tells the tale of Sofia's rich and diverse past.

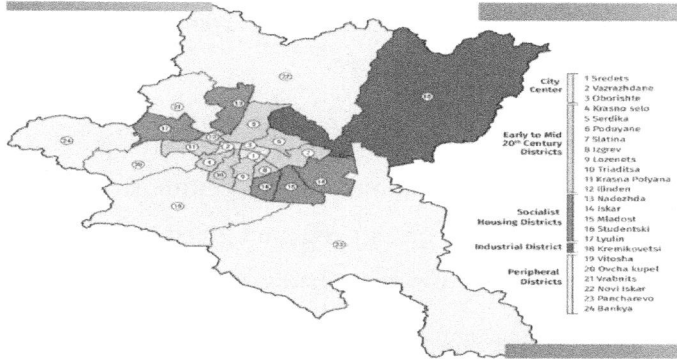

Districts of Sofia, Bulgaria

Tram in Sofia

Take a stroll down Vitosha Boulevard, the city's main shopping street, where you can find everything from high-end stores to local artisan shops.

Outdoor cafes line the boulevard, providing an ideal spot for people-watching while enjoying a rich cup of Bulgarian coffee. And if you're lucky, you might catch a live street show that adds an extra layer of vibrancy to your day.

But Sofia is not just about its picturesque streets and historic places. The city's parks and green areas offer a refreshing escape from the urban hustle.

Trees in Sofia city park (Borisova gradina), Bulgaria

Take a relaxed walk through Borisova Gradina, Sofia's oldest and most beautiful park, where you can enjoy a picnic, rent a bike, or simply relax by the lake. For a more adventurous trip, hike up Vitosha Mountain, which stands majestically on the city's outskirts, offering breathtaking views and a variety of outdoor activities.

We value your feedback!

Thank you for choosing to visit Sofia with our travel guide. We hope it enriches your journey and helps you discover the city's hidden beauties. We'd love to hear your opinions on whether you enjoyed this guide in the end! Please leave a review on Amazon. Your input benefits other travelers and inspires us to keep developing useful guides.

Happy travels, and thank you for your support!

Why Sofia in 2025?

You might be thinking, "Why Sofia in 2025?" Well, let me tell you, this city is buzzing with new attractions, revamped landmarks, and an energy that's simply tempting. Over the past few years, Sofia has experienced a significant transformation, making it one of Europe's most exciting destinations.

In 2025, Sofia is unveiling several new sites that you won't want to miss. The Sofia Skywalk, a glass-bottom walkway high above the city, offers unparalleled panoramic views that will leave you in awe. Imagine stepping onto a transparent road suspended in the air, feeling like you're walking on clouds while the city sprawls beneath you. It's a thrilling experience that's perfect for those Instagram-worthy photos.

Cultural enthusiasts will be thrilled to explore the newly opened Contemporary Art Museum, which shows cutting-edge works from local and international artists.

This dynamic location not only highlights Sofia's thriving art scene, but it also hosts interactive workshops and events that make art accessible to everyone. Assume yourself wandering through galleries filled with thought-provoking pieces, watching live art performances, and maybe even getting your hands dirty in a creative workshop.

Foodies, get ready to take on a culinary adventure. Sofia's food scene has exploded with the arrival of new farm-to-table restaurants, offering the freshest local products and innovative dishes. From traditional

Bulgarian fare to modern gastronomic treats, your taste buds are in for a treat.

Traditional Christmas food

Assume enjoying a plate of shopska salad, made with juicy tomatoes, crisp cucumbers, and creamy white cheese, or biting into a succulent piece of grilled lamb that melts in your mouth. And of course, no visit to Sofia is complete without indulging in a slice of banitsa, a delicious pastry filled with cheese that's beloved by locals and tourists alike.

In addition to its culinary wonders, Sofia is also making strides in sustainability and green living. The city has introduced new eco-friendly measures, such as expanded bike lanes, electric buses, and green spaces.

Sofia street

Assume cycling through Sofia's picturesque streets, breathing in the fresh air, and feeling positive about lowering your carbon footprint. It's a city that's not only beautiful but also forward-thinking.

Fun facts and trivia

Did you know that Sofia is one of the oldest cities in Europe, with a history that goes back over 7,000 years? That's right! Long before it became the lively capital of Bulgaria, Sofia was a thriving settlement known as Serdica.

Landmarks of Sophia - Serdica Ruins

Assume walking on streets that have watched millennia of change and evolution. Cool, isn't it? As you explore the city, you'll stumble upon remnants of its ancient past, from Roman ruins to medieval fortresses, each telling a story of a bygone age.

Here's another intriguing tidbit: Sofia is home to more than 40 mineral and thermal pools.

So, if you're a fan of hot baths and spa treatments, you're in for a treat. The city's mineral baths have been a source of health and relaxation for ages, attracting visitors seeking rejuvenation and wellness.

Assume yourself soaking in warm, mineral-rich waters, feeling the stress melt away as you relax in a historic bathhouse.

It's an experience that's both soothing and steeped in history.

Speaking of treats, did you know that Bulgaria is the world's biggest producer of rose oil? Sofia celebrates this fragrant heritage with the annual Rose Festival, a vibrant event filled with colorful parades, music, and the intoxicating scent of roses.

If you're around in May, this event is an absolute must-see. Assume strolling through fields of blooming roses, watching as the petals are harvested and distilled into precious oil, and sharing in the celebrations that celebrate this unique aspect of Bulgarian culture. But that's not all. Sofia is also known for its rich musical history.

The city's opera and ballet scene is world-renowned, with performances that match those of the most famous theaters in Europe. Assume attending a captivating opera at the National Opera and Ballet, where the powerful voices and graceful dancers take you to another world. It's an experience that will leave you spellbound and wanting for more.

And let's not forget Sofia's colorful street art. The city's walls and alleys are adorned with colorful murals and graffiti that tell stories, express social commentary, and add a splash of creativity to the urban environment. Imagine wandering through secret streets and stumbling upon stunning works of art that surprise and delight you at every turn. It's a testament to Sofia's thriving artistic community and its dedication to fostering creativity in all its forms.

With so many fascinating aspects to explore, Sofia in 2025 is a city that offers adventure, discovery, and unforgettable experiences. So, get ready to dive into its rich history, soak up its vibrant culture, and discover the hidden gems that make this city truly special.

Chapter one

Getting To Sofia

Direct flights and major airlines

Planning a trip to Sofia? Great idea! Together, we can make your trip as smooth as possible by diving into everything you need to know about direct flights and major airlines serving this vibrant city. Trust me, getting to Sofia is easier than you might think.

Why direct flights?

First things first, why should you consider direct flights? Simple: they save you time and trouble. No one likes layovers, especially when you're eager to start your adventure. Direct flights mean less hanging around, fewer chances of lost luggage, and more time to enjoy Sofia's charm.

Major Airlines Flying to Sofia Airport (SOF) is your entrance to the city. It's well-connected to many major cities around the world, thanks to a variety of airlines offering direct flights. Let's take a closer look at some of the big airlines that can whisk you away to Sofia.

Bulgaria Air

Bulgaria Air is Bulgaria's national carrier and offers a variety of direct flights from several European destinations. Think of it as your straight line into the heart of Bulgaria.

Lufthansa

Lufthansa connects Sofia to several German hubs, including Frankfurt and Munich. Lufthansa allows you to fly from the United States or other long-haul destinations to Sofia with one stop in Germany.

Ryanair and Wizz Air

These budget airlines offer numerous direct flights from various European towns. They're excellent if you're looking to save some cash. Just remember, budget airlines often come with added fees for extras like checked baggage, so plan accordingly.

British Airways

Direct flights from London to Sofia make British Airways a convenient choice for travelers coming from the UK.

Turkish Airlines

With Istanbul being a major hub, Turkish Airlines offers frequent direct flights to Sofia, making it a wonderful choice for those going from Asia, Africa, and the Middle East.

Booking your flight

When booking your ticket, it's always a beneficial idea to compare prices across different airlines. Websites like Skyscanner, Kayak, and Google Flights can help you find the best deals. And here's a pro tip: booking your flight in advance usually gets you the best deals. So, if you're planning a summer trip, start looking for flights in the spring.

Arrival at Sofia Airport

Upon landing at Sofia Airport, you'll find it's quite user-friendly. The airport has two terminals, with most international flights landing at Terminal 2.

Here's what you can expect:

Immigration and Customs: These processes are usually smooth, but it's always beneficial to have your travel documents handy.

Baggage Claim: Follow the signs to receive your luggage. If you've checked bags, they normally arrive fairly quickly.

Transportation choices: From the airport, you have several choices to get to the city center. Taxis, airport taxis, and public transportation are all available. The metro is a handy and affordable choice, taking you directly from the airport to the city in about 20 minutes.

Making the most of your flight

Long flights can be exhausting, but there are ways to make them more livable.

Here are a few tips:

Stay Hydrated: Airplane rooms can be very dry, so drink plenty of water. Avoid excessive caffeine and booze, as they can dehydrate you.

Move Around: On long trips, try to get up and stretch or walk around every couple of hours to avoid stiffness and promote circulation.

Entertainment: Bring your own entertainment. Load up your computer or e-reader with books, movies, or games. Many airlines also offer in-flight entertainment, but it's helpful to have backup choices. Comfort: Bring a neck pillow, an eye mask, and noise-canceling headphones to help you sleep and relax during the trip.

So, there you have it—everything you need to know about direct flights and big airlines to Sofia. With the right airline and a direct flight, you'll be exploring Sofia's cobblestone streets, savoring its local cuisine, and finding its hidden gems in no time.

Visa Requirements and Entry Procedures

Planning your trip to Sofia? Exciting times ahead! Before you start packing your bags, let's make sure you've got all your papers in order. Navigating visa requirements and entry procedures might sound difficult, but don't worry. I'm here to walk you through it step by step.

Do you need a visa?

First things first, do you even need a visa to enter Bulgaria? The answer depends on your country. EU/EEA Citizens: Good news! If you're a member of the European Union or the European Economic Area, you don't need a visa to enter Bulgaria. Just bring a legal passport or national ID card, and you're ready to go.

US and Canadian Citizens: Travelers from the United States and Canada can enter Bulgaria without a visa for short stays of up to 90 days within a six-month timeframe. Just make sure your passport is valid for at least three months beyond your planned departure date.

UK Citizens: Post-Brexit, UK citizens can still enter Bulgaria visa-free for short stays (up to 90 days within a six-month term). Ensure your passport is valid for at least six months after your planned travel. Other Countries: For citizens of other countries, the requirements change. Some may need a visa, while others might be qualified for visa-free entry. Check the Bulgarian Ministry of Foreign Affairs website or call your nearest Bulgarian consulate for the most accurate and up-to-date information.

Applying for a visa

If you do need a visa, don't stress. The application process is simple. Here's what you need to do: Determine Your Visa Type: Most travelers will need a short-stay visa (Type C) for tourism reasons. If you're planning a longer stay, you might need a different type of visa.

Gather your documents: Generally, you'll need:

A filled-out visa application form.

A legal passport with at least two blank pages.

Recent passport-sized photos.
Proof of travel insurance covering the entire stay.

Proof of sufficient funds (bank records or a letter from your bank).

A round-trip travel plan (flight reservations). Accommodation information (hotel booking or an invitation letter if staying with friends or family). Submit Your Application: You can apply at the Bulgarian embassy or consulate in your home country. Some countries also offer online application options. Pay the Fee: Visa fees change, so check the exact amount on the embassy's website.

Wait for Processing: Processing times can vary, but it's usually wise to apply at least a month before your planned travel dates.

Arriving in Sofia

So, you've got your visa (or confirmed you don't need one). Now, let's talk about what happens when you land in Sofia.

Immigration and Customs

Upon landing at Sofia Airport, follow the signs to immigration. Here's what you can expect: Passport Control: Have your passport and visa (if needed) ready. The officer may ask why you're visiting and where you're staying. A friendly smile and clear answers will generally do the trick.

Customs Declaration: If you're carrying more than €10,000 in cash or equivalent, you'll need to report it. There are also restrictions on certain things, like tobacco, alcohol, and food products. Check the Bulgarian customs rules beforehand to avoid any surprises.

Tips for a Smooth Entry

Be Prepared: Have all your documents (passport, visa,

trip insurance, accommodation details) easily available. Stay Calm and Friendly: Immigration officers are just doing their job. A calm and friendly attitude goes a long way.

Know the Rules: To avoid any problems, familiarize yourself with the customs rules.

Leaving Sofia

When it's time to say goodbye to Sofia, the departure process is simple. Arrive at the airport at least two hours before your flight, and follow the signs to your airline's check-in counter. After check-in, continue through security and passport control.

Transportation Options from the Airport

You've just landed at Sofia Airport, and the excitement of exploring this lively city is bubbling over. Start by traveling from the airport to Sofia's center. Don't worry, I've got you covered. Let's dive into the transportation choices available to make your journey into the city as smooth and enjoyable as possible.

Taxis: The Comfortable Option

After a long flight, sometimes you just want to get to your goal with minimal hassle. Enter the trusted taxi. Sofia's official airport taxis are a quick and comfortable way to get to the city center. They'll be right outside the arrivals area.

Quick Tips for Taking a Taxi:

Use Official Taxis: Look for the OK Supertrans badge.

Avoid touts inside the airport who might try to lure you into unofficial cabs.

Estimated Fare: A ride to the city center usually costs around 15-20 BGN (about 8–10 EUR). It's a beneficial idea to confirm the estimated fare with the driver before you start.

Payment: Most cabs accept cash only, so have some Bulgarian levs handy. Some might accept card payments, but it's best not to count on it.

Envision this: You step out of the airport, a bit drained but excited. You hop into a comfortable cab, and soon you're gliding through the streets of Sofia, the city lights flickering past as you head towards your hotel.

Easy and stress-free!

Metro: The Budget-Friendly Option

Feeling a bit more adventurous? The Sofia Metro is an excellent and cheap way to reach the city center. Plus, it's simple to use. The metro station is conveniently situated at Terminal 2. Using the Metro: Buy a ticket: Purchase a ticket at the station's vending machines or kiosks. A single ride costs 1.60 BGN (about 0.80 EUR).

Travel Time: The metro ride to the city center (Serdika Station) takes about 20–30 minutes.

Convenience: The metro runs from 5:30 AM to midnight, so unless you're flying very late at night, you should be able to catch a train.

Picture yourself navigating the clean and efficient metro system, feeling like a savvy tourist as you zip into the city center. It's a wonderful way to get a quick feel for the local vibe right from the start. Buses: For the More Adventurous Traveler If you enjoy blending in with the locals and don't mind a bit of a journey, taking the bus can be an intriguing choice. There are several bus lines that connect Sofia Airport with different parts of the city.

Bus Options:

Bus 84 runs between Terminal 1 and the city center, passing by key places. The trip takes around 45 minutes, based on traffic.

Bus 184: Similar to Bus 84 but with different stops along the way.

Practical Info:

Tickets can be purchased from kiosks or directly from the driver. They cost about 1.60 BGN (0.80 EUR).

Luggage Fee: If you have a lot of luggage, you may need to purchase an additional ticket for your bags. Envision this scenario: You're on the bus, maybe sitting next to a local who gives you some secret tips about Sofia. The bus meanders through the neighborhoods, giving you a ground-level view of the city as you near the center. It's an experience in and of itself!

Car Rentals: Freedom on Four Wheels

Planning to explore more of Bulgaria? Renting a car might be your best bet. Sofia Airport hosts several car rental companies, including foreign names like Hertz, Avis, and Europcar, as well as local agencies.

Things to consider:

Book in advance. This ensures you get the best deals and availability.

Driving in Bulgaria: Familiarize yourself with the area's driving laws and road conditions.

Navigation: A GPS or a reliable map app is important, especially if you plan to explore beyond Sofia. You can use tools like Google Maps to help you get around.

Envision the freedom of having your own set of wheels. You can start your adventure right from the airport, perhaps by taking a scenic drive up to Vitosha Mountain or making a day trip to the historic Rila Monastery.

Ride-sharing: The Modern Way

Prefer the ease of ride-sharing? Apps like Uber and Bolt run in Sofia. Just fire up the app, request a ride, and you'll be on your way.

So, there you have it—everything you need to know about going from Sofia Airport to the city center.

Whether you choose the comfort of a taxi, the affordability of the metro, the local taste of the bus, the freedom of a rental car, or the convenience of a ride-sharing app, Sofia has got you covered. Safe travels, and welcome to this beautiful city!

Traveler Steves

Chapter two

Insider Tips for a Memorable Journey

The best times to visit

Choosing the best time to visit Sofia can make a big difference in your travel experience. Whether you're looking to soak up the sun, enjoy cultural festivals, or hit the ski slopes, Sofia has something to offer year-round. Let's explore the best times to visit Sofia, considering weather conditions, activities, and budget-friendly choices for each season.

Spring: A Blooming Delight (March to May)

Spring in Sofia is like a breath of fresh air. As the city shakes off the winter chill, flowers bloom and parks come alive with color. The temperatures are mild, ranging from 10°C (50°F) to 20°C (68°F), making it ideal for exploring the city on foot.

Why visit in the spring?

Cherry Blossoms: Yes, Sofia has its own cherry blossom season! Borisova Gradina and South Park are beautiful places to watch this floral spectacle.

Easter Celebrations: If you visit around Orthodox Easter, you'll get to experience traditional Bulgarian customs and lively church services.

Less Crowded: Spring is before the peak tourist season, so you can enjoy the sites without the crowds.

Budget-Friendly: Accommodation prices are usually lower than in the summer, making it a favorable time for budget-conscious travelers.

Envision strolling through a blooming garden, with the smell of flowers in the air and a light breeze on your face. Doesn't that sound idyllic?

Summer: Festivals and Sunshine (June to August)

Summer is the peak tourist season in Sofia. The city buzzes with energy, and there's always something going on. Temperatures range from 25°C (77°F) to 35°C (95°F), so pack light clothes and stay hydrated.

Why visit in the summer?

Vitosha Mountain is just a short drive from the city, offering hiking tracks and cool retreats from the summer heat.

Cultural events: Sofia is alive with music, theater, and dance events. The Sofia Opera and Ballet season also peaks in the summer.

Outdoor cafes and restaurants in the city are in full swing. Enjoy a relaxed meal while people-watching on Vitosha Boulevard.

Extended Daylight: Longer days mean more time to explore and enjoy the city's highlights.

Think of it: basking in the summer sun, having a cold drink at an outdoor café, and soaking in the vibrant atmosphere. Summer in Sofia is simply amazing.

Autumn: A Golden Experience (September to November)

Autumn is a wonderful time to visit Sofia. The temperatures cool down to a reasonable range of 10°C (50°F) to 20°C (68°F), and the fall foliage is spectacular. The city's parks and nearby countryside turn into a painter's palette of reds, oranges, and yellows.

Why visit in the autumn?

Wine Harvest Season: Bulgaria's winemaking heritage is rich. Visit nearby wineries and enjoy wine-tasting tours.
Sofia Film Festival: This is a must for movie buffs. The festival features both local and international films.
Pleasant Weather: The cooler temperatures are ideal for exploring Sofia's historic sites and museums.

Budget-Friendly: Like spring, autumn attracts fewer tourists, resulting in lower accommodation prices and fewer groups.

Envision sipping on a glass of Bulgarian wine, surrounded by the golden hues of fall leaves. It's a serene and beautiful time to be in Sofia.

Winter: A Cozy Wonderland (December to February)
Winter in Sofia can be chilly, with temps often dropping below freezing. But don't let that stop you!

Winter turns the city into a cozy wonderland, and there are plenty of indoor and outdoor activities to enjoy.

Why visit during the winter?

Christmas Markets: Sofia's Christmas markets are lovely and festive, filled with local crafts, food, and mulled wine.

Skiing on Vitosha: Just a stone's throw from the city,

Vitosha Mountain offers skiing and snowboarding. It's a wonderful day trip for winter sports enthusiasts.

Thermal Baths: Warm up and relax in Sofia's mineral baths, a wonderful way to recover after a day of exploring.

Budget-Friendly: Winter is off-peak for tourists (except around Christmas), so you can find excellent deals on flights and accommodations.

Envision this: wrapped in a warm coat, strolling through a festive market, a cup of hot cocoa in hand, as snowflakes slowly fall around you. Winter in Sofia is magical.

Weather and Budget Considerations

Understanding Sofia's weather patterns and budget effects for each season can help you plan the perfect trip.

Spring Weather and Budget:

Weather: mild and pleasant, perfect for outdoor activities.

Budget: Affordable, with lower lodging and flight prices than in summer.

Summer Weather and Budget:

Weather: hot and sunny, ideal for outdoor festivals and activities.

Budget: higher, as it's the peak travel season. Book rooms and flights well in advance to get the best deals.

Autumn Weather and Budget:

Weather: cool and comfortable, with beautiful fall scenery.

Budget: Moderate, with fewer tourists and more options in hotels and flights.

Winter Weather and Budget:

Weather: cold, with chances of snow. Ideal for winter sports and festive events.

Budget: lower, except around the Christmas and New Year breaks. Great deals can be found, especially for early bookers.

Finding your perfect time

So, when is the best time to visit Sofia? It really depends on what you're looking for. For mild weather and beautiful parks, spring is your best bet.

If you love festivals and outdoor activities, summer is great.
Autumn brings beautiful foliage and a relaxed atmosphere.
Winter is an ideal time for festive markets and winter sports.

No matter when you decide to visit Sofia, this city will welcome you with open arms and a wealth of adventures. Each season brings its own charm and unique activities. So, pick the time that suits your preferences, pack accordingly, and get ready to make unforgettable memories in Sofia. Safe travels, and enjoy every moment!

Local etiquette and customs

Whether you're wandering the bustling streets, savoring delicious Bulgarian food, or mingling with the locals, understanding Sofia's etiquette and customs can make your experience even more enjoyable. Let's dive into the cultural details that will help you connect with the heart of this vibrant city.

Greetings and introductions

In Sofia, greetings are more than just a formality—they're a way of showing respect and warmth.

Common Greetings:

In formal settings, a firm handshake with eye contact is the standard greeting. It's a sign of respect and earnestness. Picture this: you meet a local, extend your hand for a confident shake, and instantly set a positive tone for the interaction. It's a small act, but it can go a long way toward making a favorable impression.

Kisses on the Cheek: Among friends and family, a kiss on each cheek is customary. It's a warm and personal way to meet someone you're close to. But don't worry; if you're not sure, a friendly smile works just fine. Presume you're introduced to a friend's family at a cozy dinner; you might be met with this affectionate gesture, and it's totally okay to reciprocate or simply smile.

Addressing People:

Titles are important in Bulgarian culture. When addressing someone, especially in a formal setting, it's polite to use their title and last name until they ask you to use their first name.

Example:
Formal: "Mr. Ivanov" or "Mrs. Dimitrova" After getting to know them better, say "Ivan" or "Maria."

It's similar to how you'd treat a professor or a new

boss—start formal and let them guide you to informality.

Table Manners

Dining in Sofia is a delightful experience, and learning a bit about local table manners can make it even better.

Dining Etiquette:

Wait to Be Seated: If you're eating in a restaurant, wait for the host to show you to your table. It's a small but important sign of respect.

Toast with Rakia: Rakia, a native fruit brandy, is often used for toasts. Wait for the host to make the first toast before sipping your drink. It's a moment to stop and share a collective cheer with those around you.

Finish Your Plate: It's considered polite to finish the food on your plate, showing respect for the meal. Picture yourself at a cozy Bulgarian restaurant. The waiter brings out a plate of shopska salad, and you wait a moment to see if a toast is coming. It's these little touches that help you fit right in.

Dress Code

Bulgarians usually dress well, especially in urban areas like Sofia. While casual wear is fine for sightseeing, consider dressing a bit more formally for dining out or visiting events.

What to wear:

Daytime: comfortable yet stylish clothes. Think smart-casual.
Evening: Slightly more formal clothing, like a stylish dress or a collared shirt.

Presume blending in with the locals; your outfit shows the city's stylish yet laid-back vibe. It's an easy way to show respect for the local culture.

Personal space and behavior

Understanding personal space and behavior in Sofia

can help you escape unintentional faux pas.
Personal Space:

Proximity: Bulgarians tend to stand a bit closer during conversations than what might be normal in some other cultures. It's a sign of friendliness, not harassment.

movements: Avoid pointing directly at people or using overly expressive hand movements, as this can be seen as impolite.

Think of it as having a friendly chat with a friend. Closeness is about relationships, not discomfort.

Gift Giving

If you're called to a Bulgarian home, bringing a small gift is a lovely gesture.

Gift Ideas:

Flowers: Always an excellent choice, but remember to give an odd number of flowers (even numbers are for funerals).

Sweets or Wine: A box of chocolates or a bottle of good wine will be welcomed.

Presume showing up with a beautiful bouquet or a delicious box of chocolates. It's a simple way to show gratitude and respect for your host's hospitality.

Respect for traditions

Bulgaria is rich in traditions, and showing respect for these can deepen your relationship with Sofia.

Key Traditions:

Martenitsa: In March, Bulgarians share red and white yarn ornaments for health and happiness. Wearing them is a charming way to connect with the culture. Name Days: Many Bulgarians celebrate their Name Day (a celebration of the saint they are named after) more than their birthday. A simple "Happy Name Day" can mean a lot.

Presume wearing a martenitsa on your wrist—a small

yet important gesture that shows you're embracing the local customs.

Tipping

Tipping in Sofia is customary, though not required. It's a way to show thanks for excellent service.

Tipping Guidelines:

a) Restaurants: Leave around 10% of the bill.
b) Taxis: You are welcome to round up to the nearest whole number.
c) Hotels: A small tip for the housekeeping staff is a thoughtful offering.
d) Think of tipping as a way to say "thank you" for outstanding service, just as you might back home.

Navigating Sofia with an understanding of local etiquette and customs will enrich your experience and help you build important connections. Whether you're sharing a meal, exploring the city, or engaging with locals, these small acts of respect and cultural knowledge can make a big difference.

Money-Saving Tips

Sofia has plenty of ways to help you stretch your euros, dollars, or leva.

Plan ahead and be flexible.

Advance Booking: Planning your trip in advance is one of the best ways to save money. Booking flights, accommodations, and even some activities ahead of time can often get you the best deals. Airlines and hotels frequently offer early bird savings.

Flexibility: If you can be flexible with your travel dates, you might find cheaper choices. Mid-week flights and stays are generally less expensive than weekends. Plus, visiting during the shoulder seasons (spring and fall) can offer favorable weather without the high prices of peak seasons.

Accommodation Tips

Sofia has a wide range of budget-friendly hotels and hostels. Hostels are not only cheap but also a wonderful way to meet fellow tourists. Look for deals on booking services, and consider staying in a private room in a hostel if you prefer some privacy.

Short-Term Rentals: Platforms like Airbnb can offer excellent deals, especially for longer stays. Sometimes renting an apartment can be cheaper than staying in a hotel, and you get the added benefit of having a kitchen to make your own meals.

Membership Programs: If you travel frequently, consider joining a hotel membership program. Accumulating points can lead to free nights or improvements.

Eating and drinking on a budget

Shopping at local markets like the Women's Market or the Central Market Hall is a wonderful way to save money and enjoy fresh, local food. Grab some wonderful Bulgarian cheese, fresh bread, and seasonal fruits for a picnic.

Street Food: Don't miss out on Sofia's street food. You can get a filling banitsa (a traditional pastry) for breakfast or lunch at a fraction of the cost of a restaurant meal.

Lunch Deals: Many restaurants offer lunch specials that are significantly less expensive than their dinner menus. Look out for these deals and enjoy a fantastic meal at a lower price.

Tap water in Sofia is safe to drink, so bring a filled water bottle and save money (and the environment) by not buying bottled water.

Getting Around

Sofia's public transportation system is efficient and very affordable. A single ticket for the metro, trains, or buses costs just a few levs. Consider getting a day pass or a multi-day pass if you plan to use public transportation frequently.

Walking: Sofia is a very walkable city. Most of the main sites are within walking distance of each other, so you can save money and enjoy the city at a leisurely pace.
Bike Rentals: Getting a bike is another cheap and enjoyable way to get around. There are several bike rental services in the city, and it's an excellent way to explore Sofia's parks and bike-friendly places.

Free and low-cost activities

Free Walking Tours: Sofia gives several free walking tours. These tours are a fantastic way to get to know the city's past and culture.

While the tours are free, tipping the guide at the end is welcome.
Parks and Outdoor Spaces: For free, enjoy Sofia's many beautiful parks, such as Borisova Gradina and South Park. They are ideal for a relaxing day out, a picnic, or some light exercise.

Museums and Galleries: Many of Sofia's museums and

galleries have free entry days or discounted rates. Check their websites for special deals.

Neighborhood events: Keep an eye out for free neighborhood events, concerts, and festivals. Sofia has a vibrant culture scene with many free or low-cost events, especially during the summer months. Smart money management.

Currency Exchange: Avoid exchanging money at the airport, where rates are generally worse. Instead, use the city's ATMs to get local currency. Most ATMs in Sofia offer fair exchange rates.

Credit Cards and Cash: While credit cards are generally accepted in Sofia, it's a good idea to carry some cash for small purchases, tips, and places that don't accept cards.

Budget Tracking Apps: Use budgeting apps to keep track of your costs. Apps like Trail Wallet or Mint can help you monitor your spending and stay within your limit.

Loans and savings

Savings: Building up savings before your trip can give you peace of mind and a little extra cushion for unexpected costs. Setting aside a small amount daily can add up quickly.

Travel Loans: If you need a loan to pay for your trip, shop around for the best rates and terms. Some banks give travel-specific loans, but be cautious and ensure you can comfortably repay the loan after your trip.

Traveling to Sofia doesn't have to be expensive. With a bit of planning and these money-saving tips, you can enjoy everything this wonderful city has to offer without hurting your budget. Remember, the best experiences often come from the simplest joys, like wandering through a park, savoring local street food, or chatting with a local over a cup of coffee.

Apps and Resources for Travelers

Making the Most of Your Sofia Adventure

Planning a trip to Sofia is exciting, but exploring a new city can sometimes feel overwhelming. Fear not! With the right apps and tools, you can turn your phone into a handy travel companion, ensuring you make the most of your time in this vibrant city. Here's everything you need to know about the best apps, links, and tools to help you explore Sofia like a pro.

Essential travel apps

Google Maps First things first, you'll need an accurate map. In Sofia, Google Maps is your best friend. It's useful for navigating the city, finding attractions, and even discovering hidden gems.

Features: real-time navigation; public transport plans; restaurant reviews.

Link: Google Maps

Fancy you've just stepped out of a café, wanting a historical adventure. Google Maps will guide you to the old Serdica ruins, just a few blocks away.

Citymapper: Citymapper is a useful app for getting around Sofia using public transportation. It gives detailed directions, including bus, tram, and metro schedules, and it's very user-friendly. Features: step-by-step navigation, real-time departure details, service disruption alerts.

Link: Citymapper:

https://citymapper.com/directions?endcoord=51.537060%2C-0.079179&endname=The%20Proud%20Archivist&endaddress=2-10%20Hertford%20Road%2C%20London%2C%20N1%205ET

Picture this: You're trying to get to the National Palace of Culture. Citymapper tells you exactly which train to take and when it will arrive.

TripAdvisor: TripAdvisor is your go-to app for reviews and suggestions on hotels, restaurants, and attractions. It's a wonderful way to see what other tourists are saying and find the best spots in Sofia.

Features: user reviews, photos, booking choices, forums.

Link: TripAdvisor: [Check out reviews on TripAdvisor](https://www.tripadvisor.com/Restaurant_

You're looking for the best place to try traditional Bulgarian food. TripAdvisor points you to a lovely local restaurant with rave reviews. Bon appétit! XE Currency Converter Managing your money while traveling is important, and XE Currency Converter helps you keep track of exchange rates and conversions on the go.

Features: real-time currency conversion, past rate charts, offline mode.

Link: XE Currency Converter:

https://www.xe.com/currencyconverter/

Fancy you're shopping at a local market and want to know how much those beautiful handmade souvenirs will cost in your home currency. XE has got you covered.

Google Translate While many people in Sofia speak English, it's always helpful to have a translation app on hand. Google Translate can help you interact with and understand signs, menus, and more.

Features: text translation, voice translation, offline mode, quick camera translation.

Picture this: you're at a local restaurant, and you want to try something new but can't read the menu. It is translated immediately by Google Translates camera function, and you can place an order with confidence.

Local insights and cultural resources

Visit Sofia The main tourism website for Sofia is packed with information on attractions, events, and practical tips. It's a useful resource for planning your schedule.

Features: event calendars, attraction guides, and trip tips.

Link: Visit Sofia:

https://www.visitsofia.bg/en/

Fancy you're looking for festivals or special events going on during your stay. Visit Sofia has all the latest information and details.

Sofia Urban Mobility Center For detailed information about public transportation, ticket prices, and routes, the Sofia Urban Mobility Center website is essential. Features: public transport routes, schedules, and fare details.

Link: Sofia Urban Mobility Center:

https://www.sofiatraffic.bg/en

You want to plan a day to visit different parts of Sofia using public transit. This site helps you map out your trip efficiently.

BG Menu If you're in the mood to relax at your accommodation and order in, BG Menu is a popular food delivery service in Sofia. Browse menus from a variety of restaurants and have your meal brought to your home.

Features: wide range of restaurants; online ordering; delivery tracking.

Link: BG Menu: https://www.takeaway.com/bg/

Picture this: after a long day of sightseeing, you're too exhausted to go out for dinner. The BG Menu brings the best of Sofia's culinary scene right to you.

Keeping connected and safe

WhatsApp Stay in touch with friends and family back home or meet with fellow travelers using WhatsApp. It's a wonderful way to share your travels in real time. Features: free texting, voice and video calls, group chats.

Fancy sharing a stunning photo of Alexander Nevsky Cathedral with your family immediately after returning home. WhatsApp makes it easy.

Revolut For managing your finances and making

international transactions without hefty fees, Revolut is a fantastic choice. It's particularly useful for travelers. Features: multi-currency accounts; fee-free shopping; instant currency exchange.

Link: Revolut: https://www.revolut.com/

You're at a restaurant and ready to pay your bill. Revolut lets you do so without worrying about hidden fees, keeping your travel spending in check.

Sofia Public Safety Stay informed about area safety updates and emergency contacts. Bookmarking the Sofia Public Safety page can provide peace of mind. Features: emergency numbers, safety tips, and neighborhood alerts.

Link: Sofia Public Safety:

https://www.sofia.bg/web/sofia-municipality

It's always beneficial to have a backup plan. Knowing where to find emergency information ensures you're prepared for any case.

This app and tools set will help you maximize your Sofia stay. From navigating the city and finding the best restaurants to managing your money and staying connected, these tools will help you explore with confidence and ease. So, download a few of these apps, bookmark those links, and get ready for an amazing adventure in Sofia.

Traveler Steves

Chapter three

Where To Stay in Sofia

Top hotels and accommodations

Sense Hotel Sofia

Why choose the Sense Hotel? Picture this: You're stepping into a sleek, contemporary lobby that quickly makes you feel like you've arrived somewhere special. This isn't just a place to sleep; it's an adventure. Sense Hotel is known for its impeccable design, personalized service, and prime location. Whether you're a work traveler or a tourist, you'll find that the attention to detail here makes all the difference.

Location

Situated on the iconic Tsar Osvoboditel Boulevard, the Sense Hotel boasts an unbeatable setting. You're just stepping away from some of Sofia's most famous sites, including the Alexander Nevsky Cathedral and the Bulgarian Parliament. The central location means you can explore the city with ease, whether you're on foot, using public transport, or taking a short cab ride.

Room Types and Features

Sense Hotel offers a variety of room types to meet every traveler's needs:

Standard Rooms: cozy and stylish, ideal for solo travelers or couples.

Superior Rooms: extra space and city views, ideal for those who want a little more luxury.

Executive Rooms: Business travelers will enjoy the extra amenities and workspace.

Suites: For the ultimate indulgence, the suites offer expansive living rooms, stunning views, and all the comforts of home.

Each room features modern decor, plush carpeting, high-speed Wi-Fi, and a smart TV. Fancy unwinding in a spacious room, sipping on a complimentary espresso from your in-room Nespresso machine, and looking out at the city skyline. It's the right blend of relaxation and sophistication.

Amenities

The Sense Hotel Sofia offers more than just rooms; it also provides an experience. Here are some of the standout amenities:

Rooftop Bar: Enjoy panoramic views of Sofia while sipping on a craft drink. It's a favorite spot for both guests and locals.

Spa and Wellness Center: Pamper yourself with a massage, rest in the sauna, or take a dip in the indoor pool.

Fitness Center: Stay on top of your workout program with state-of-the-art equipment.

Business Facilities: Meeting rooms and a business center are fully prepared to accommodate corporate guests.

Concierge Service: Need passes to a show, a dinner reservation, or a city tour? The concierge is there to help.

Dining Options

Dining at the Sense Hotel is a sensory delight. The hotel's restaurant offers a diverse menu of foreign and Bulgarian cuisine, made with fresh, locally sourced ingredients. Start your day with a delicious breakfast spread, enjoy a leisurely lunch, or indulge in a gourmet dinner. The rooftop bar also serves a selection of light bites and tapas, making it ideal for a casual evening with friends.

Pricing

Sense Hotel Sofia offers luxury accommodations at a range of prices, based on the season and room type. Standard rooms usually start at around €150 per night, while suites can go up to €400 per night. Keep an eye out for special offers and packages, especially if you book straight through the hotel's website.

Guest Reviews

Guests rave about their adventures at Sense Hotel Sofia. Common praises include the exceptional service, stylish decor, and prime position. Many reviewers highlight the rooftop bar as a must-visit spot, and the spa facilities receive high marks for offering a relaxing retreat in the heart of the city.

Unique Selling Points

What sets the Sense Hotel apart from other luxury hotels in Sofia?

Rooftop Bar: One of the city's best views.

Central Location: Walking distance to major attractions.

Design: modern, sleek, and sophisticated furnishings. Service: A personalized and careful service that makes you feel at home.

Booking Information

Booking a stay at the Sense Hotel is simple. You can book straight through their official website for the best rates and special offers. This hotel is also listed on major booking platforms, such as Booking.com and Expedia.

Nearby Attractions

Staying at the Sense Hotel puts you in close proximity to some of Sofia's top attractions:

Alexander Nevsky Church: A short walk away, this stunning church is a must-see.

Bulgarian Parliament: Explore the history and design of this important building.

Sofia University is one of the oldest and most prestigious universities in Bulgaria.

Vitosha Boulevard is the main shopping and dining street in Sofia, ideal for an evening stroll.

Transportation and accessibility

Sense Hotel is easily accessible, whether you're coming by plane, train, or car.

From Sofia Airport: The hotel is about a 15-minute drive from the airport. You can take a taxi or plan for the hotel's private transfer service.

Public Transport: The closest metro station, Sofia University, is just a few minutes' walk away.

Parking: The hotel provides valet parking for guests arriving by car.

Contact Information

For more information or to make a reservation, please call Sense Hotel Sofia directly:

Address: 16 Tsar Osvoboditel Blvd., Sofia, Bulgaria
Phone: +359 2 446 24 00
Email: info@sensehotel.com
Website: Sense Hotel Sofia

The Sense Hotel Sofia is more than just a place to stay; it's a location in and of itself. With its prime location, luxurious amenities, and exceptional service, it's the perfect base for discovering everything Sofia has to offer. Whether you're here for a weekend getaway, a business trip, or a longer vacation, Sense Hotel offers a memorable and indulgent experience.

2. InterContinental Sofia

Discovering Elegance and Comfort in Sofia

Why choose InterContinental Sofia? Fancy stepping into a grand lobby with sophisticated decor and being met by friendly staff who are ready to cater to your every need. This hotel is not just a place to stay; it's an adventure. Known for its excellent service, luxurious rooms, and central location, the InterContinental Sofia offers everything you need for a memorable stay.

Location

The InterContinental Sofia, located on the famous Narodno Sabranie Square, offers an enviable location. You're just stepping away from important landmarks such as the Alexander Nevsky Cathedral and the Bulgarian Parliament. This prime spot means you can quickly explore Sofia's rich history and vibrant culture right from your doorstep.

Room Types and Features

InterContinental Sofia offers a variety of room types to meet different preferences and needs.

Classic Rooms: stylish and comfortable, ideal for solo travelers or pairs.

Executive Rooms: Featuring extra amenities and access to the Club InterContinental Lounge, perfect for business travelers.

Suites: spacious and luxurious, with separate living rooms and stunning views of the city.

Each room is designed with elegance and comfort in mind, with plush bedding, high-speed Wi-Fi, smart TVs, and modern bathrooms. Picture yourself relaxing in a cozy armchair, sipping on a cup of freshly brewed coffee from your in-room espresso machine, and enjoying the view of the lively city below.

Amenities

InterContinental Sofia offers a range of amenities to make your stay as simple and enjoyable as possible: Club InterContinental Lounge: Exclusive access for guests staying in Executive Rooms and Suites, offering complimentary breakfast, refreshments, and evening cocktails.

Fitness Center: Fully equipped with state-of-the-art tools for those who want to stay active during their stay.

Spa Services: Indulge in a variety of spa treatments meant to relax and rejuvenate.

Business Facilities: modern meeting rooms and a business center stocked with everything you need for a productive stay.

Concierge Service: Whether you need dinner reservations, tickets to a show, or recommendations for area attractions, the concierge team is there to help.

Dining Options

Dining at the InterContinental Sofia is a culinary treat. The hotel offers several dining options that cater to different tastes and occasions:

Floret Restaurant and Bar: Offering a menu of foreign and Bulgarian dishes, this stylish restaurant is perfect for a casual meal or a special dinner.

Gourmet Lounge: A cozy spot to enjoy light bites, pastries, and a range of teas and coffees throughout the day.

Club InterContinental Lounge: Exclusive for Executive Room and Suite guests, offering complimentary food and drinks in a refined setting.

Fancy starting your day with a delicious breakfast at Floret, having a leisurely lunch at the Gourmet Lounge, and finishing the evening with a cocktail in the Club InterContinental Lounge.

Pricing

InterContinental Sofia offers luxury accommodations at a range of prices, based on the season and room type. Classic rooms usually start around €200 per night, while suites can go up to €500 per night. Look out for special packages and deals, especially if you book straight through the hotel's website.

Guest Reviews

Guests constantly praise the InterContinental Sofia for its excellent service, luxurious rooms, and prime location. Many highlight the comfortable beds, delicious breakfast choices, and attentive staff. The Club InterContinental Lounge is often mentioned as a standout feature, offering an exclusive and relaxing environment for guests.

Unique Selling Points

What makes InterContinental Sofia stand out from other luxury hotels in the city?

Prime Location: Situated in the heart of Sofia, close to major sites.

Club InterContinental Lounge: Exclusive access to a refined area with complimentary food and drinks. Exceptional Service: A personalized service that makes every guest feel special.

Elegant Design: modern, stylish rooms and shared areas that provide a luxurious atmosphere.

Booking Information

Booking a stay at the InterContinental Sofia is easy. You can book straight through their official website for the best rates and special offers. This hotel is also listed on major booking websites, such as Booking.com and Expedia.

Nearby Attractions

Staying at InterContinental Sofia puts you within walking distance of some of Sofia's most popular attractions:

Alexander Nevsky Cathedral is a stunning architectural wonder, just a short walk away.

Bulgarian Parliament: Explore the history and architecture of this important building.

Ivan Vazov National Theatre: Enjoy a play or simply enjoy the beautiful exterior.

Vitosha Boulevard: Sofia's main shopping and dining street, ideal for an evening stroll.

Transportation and accessibility

InterContinental Sofia is easily accessible, whether you're coming by plane, train, or car.

From Sofia Airport: The hotel is about a 20-minute drive from the airport. You can take a taxi or plan for the hotel's private transfer service.

Public Transport: The nearest metro station, Serdika, is a short walk away, allowing quick access to other parts of the city.

Parking: The hotel provides valet parking for guests arriving by car.

Contact Information

For more information or to make a reservation, you can call InterContinental Sofia directly:

Address: 4 Narodno Sabranie Square, Sofia, Bulgaria.
Phone: +359 2 933 4334
Email: info@ihg.com
Website: InterContinental Sofia

InterContinental Sofia offers an unparalleled mix of luxury, comfort, and convenience in the heart of Sofia. With its prime location, elegant rooms, top-notch services, and exceptional service, it's the perfect base for exploring everything Sofia has to offer. Whether you're in town for work or leisure, InterContinental Sofia promises a memorable and indulgent experience.

3. Grand Hotel Sofia

Why choose the Grand Hotel Sofia? Fancy stepping into a world where timeless elegance meets modern comfort. This isn't just a place to rest your head; it's a location in itself. Known for its spacious rooms, refined decor, and excellent service, the Grand Hotel Sofia provides everything you need for a memorable stay. Whether you're attending a meeting or exploring the city, you'll find that the hotel's attention to detail enhances every moment of your visit.

Location

The Grand Hotel Sofia is perfectly located on the corner of General Gurko Street and Vasil Levski Boulevard, giving quick access to the city's main attractions. You're just a short walk away from sites like the Ivan Vazov National Theatre, the National Art Gallery, and the bustling Vitosha Boulevard. This prime location means you can immerse yourself in Sofia's rich culture and lively atmosphere right from the moment you step outside.

Room Types and Features

The hotel offers a range of room types to cater to different needs and preferences.

Classic Rooms: Elegant and comfortable, ideal for solo travelers or couples wanting a cozy retreat.

Deluxe Rooms: Offering more room and enhanced amenities, they are ideal for those looking for extra comfort.

Executive Rooms: Featuring extra workspaces and executive amenities, they are ideal for business travelers.

Suites: Luxuriously appointed with separate living areas and stunning views, offering the ultimate in comfort and style.

Each room is equipped with plush bedding, high-speed Wi-Fi, flat-screen TVs, and roomy bathrooms. Envision unwinding after a long day in a beautifully appointed room, sinking into a comfortable bed, and having a peaceful night's sleep.

Amenities

The Grand Hotel Sofia offers a range of amenities meant to make your stay as enjoyable and convenient as possible.

Fitness Center: Keep up with your workout program with state-of-the-art equipment.

Spa Services: Relax and rejuvenate with a range of spa treatments and massages.

Business Facilities: Modern meeting rooms and a fully equipped business center cater to all your professional needs.

Concierge Service: From dinner reservations to city tours, the concierge team is ready to help with all your plans.

Dining Options

Dining at the Grand Hotel Sofia is an event in itself. The hotel features several dining choices that cater to various tastes and occasions: Shades of Red Restaurant offers a sophisticated menu of foreign and Bulgarian cuisine, perfect for a special dinner or a business lunch.

Triaditza Restaurant: Enjoy a rich breakfast buffet or a lovely lunch in a stylish setting.

The Terrace is a seasonal outdoor venue that offers light meals and drinks with stunning views over the city.

Grand Café: A cozy spot for coffee, pastries, and small snacks throughout the day.

Envision starting your day with a delicious breakfast on The Terrace, having a leisurely lunch at Triaditza Restaurant, and ending the evening with a gourmet dinner at Shades of Red.

Pricing

The Grand Hotel Sofia offers luxurious accommodations at reasonable prices. Classic rooms usually start around €150 per night, while suites can range up to €400 per night. Keep an eye out for special offers and packages, especially if you book straight through the hotel's website.

Guest Reviews

Guests regularly praise the Grand Hotel Sofia for its spacious rooms, exceptional service, and central location. Many note the elegant decor, comfortable beds, and quality of the dining choices. The attentive and helpful staff often receive commendations for making guests feel welcome and well cared for.

Unique Selling Points

What sets the Grand Hotel Sofia apart from other luxury hotels in the city?

Spacious Rooms: Some of the largest hotel rooms in Sofia give plenty of space to relax and unwind. Central Location: Close to important attractions, shopping, and dining areas.

Elegant Design: A mix of classic and modern styles that provides a luxurious ambiance.

Exceptional Service: personalized care that ensures a comfortable and enjoyable stay.

Booking Information

Booking a stay at the Grand Hotel Sofia is simple. You can book straight through their official website for the best rates and special offers. This hotel is also listed on major booking websites, such as Booking.com and Expedia.

Nearby Attractions

Staying at the Grand Hotel Sofia puts you within easy reach of some of Sofia's top attractions:

The Ivan Vazov National Theatre is a beautiful historic building and a hub for cultural events. National Art Gallery: Explore Bulgaria's rich artistic history.

Alexander Nevsky Cathedral is one of Sofia's most iconic sites.

Vitosha Boulevard is the main shopping and dining street in Sofia, ideal for an evening stroll.

Transportation and accessibility

The Grand Hotel Sofia is easily accessible, whether you're coming by plane, train, or car.

From Sofia Airport: The hotel is about a 20-minute drive from the airport. You can take a taxi or plan for the hotel's private transfer service.

Public Transport: The nearest metro station, Serdika, is a short walk away, allowing quick access to other parts of the city.

Parking: The hotel offers secure underground parking for guests coming by car.

Contact Information

For more information or to make a reservation, you can call Grand Hotel Sofia directly:

Address: 1 Gurko Street, Sofia, Bulgaria.
Phone: +359 2 811 0811
Email: reservations@grandhotelsofia.bg
Grand Hotel Sofia's website

The Grand Hotel Sofia blends the charm of classic luxury with the comforts of modern amenities, all in a prime location in the heart of Sofia. With spacious rooms, exquisite dining options, and exceptional service, it's the perfect base for exploring everything this lively city has to offer. Whether you're in town for work or leisure, the Grand Hotel Sofia promises a memorable and indulgent experience. Book your stay today and discover the elegance and kindness that make this hotel a standout choice in Sofia.

The Best Western Premier Sofia Airport Hotel

Why choose the Best Western Premier Sofia Airport Hotel? Envision getting off a long flight and arriving at your hotel within minutes. No long taxi rides, no stress—just a smooth transition from air travel to relaxation. This hotel is ideal for business travelers, layovers, or anyone who values proximity to the airport without sacrificing comfort and amenities.

Location

Situated just 1 kilometer from Sofia Airport, the Best Western Premier Sofia Airport Hotel offers unparalleled convenience for visitors. The hotel offers a complimentary shuttle service to and from the airport, making your journey even smoother. Plus, you're just a short drive away from Sofia's city center, where you can enjoy the rich history and vibrant culture of Bulgaria's capital.

Room Types and Features

The hotel offers a range of room types to suit different needs and preferences.

Standard Rooms: comfortable and well-equipped, ideal for short stays.

Superior Rooms: Providing extra space and additional amenities for a more comfortable stay.

Executive Rooms: Designed with business travelers in mind, they have workspaces and improved services.

Suites: spacious and luxurious, with separate living rooms and premium amenities.

Each room is designed with modern decor and includes plush bedding, high-speed Wi-Fi, flat-screen TVs, and well-appointed bathrooms. Envision sinking into a comfortable bed after a long trip, knowing you're just minutes from the airport and ready for whatever the next day brings.

Amenities

The Best Western Premier Sofia Airport Hotel offers a range of amenities to ensure a pleasant and productive stay.
Fitness Center: Stay active with state-of-the-art exercise equipment provided 24/7.

Business Center: Fully equipped with computers, printers, and meeting rooms to cater to your business needs.

Conference Facilities: Modern and versatile areas ideal for meetings, conferences, and events.

Complimentary Airport Shuttle: Convenient and reliable travel to and from Sofia Airport.

Free Wi-Fi: high-speed internet service throughout the hotel to keep you connected.

Dining Options

Dining at the Best Western Premier Sofia Airport Hotel is a delight, with several choices to suit your culinary cravings:

Barillon 1909 Restaurant offers a diverse menu of foreign and Bulgarian cuisine, perfect for any meal of the day. Start your morning with a hearty breakfast spread, enjoy a business lunch, or savor a leisurely dinner.

Lobby Bar: A cozy spot to relax with a drink and light snacks after a busy day of travel or meetings. Envision having a delicious meal at Barillon 1909, where the menu caters to both local flavors and international tastes, ensuring there's something for everyone.

Pricing

The Best Western Premier Sofia Airport Hotel offers reasonable rates, especially given its proximity to the airport and range of amenities. Standard rooms usually start at around €90 per night, while suites can go up to €200 per night. Look out for special deals and packages on the hotel's website or big booking platforms.

Guest Reviews

Guests frequently praise the hotel for its excellent location, friendly staff, and clean, comfy rooms. The complimentary shuttle service and modern amenities also score high marks. Many reviewers appreciate the ease of being close to the airport while still having a high standard of accommodation and service.

Unique Selling Points

What makes the Best Western Premier Sofia Airport Hotel stand out from other airport hotels? Proximity to the Airport: With a free shuttle service, you're just 1 kilometer away.

Modern Amenities: From the fitness center to the business facilities, everything is built for convenience and comfort.

Exceptional Service: Attentive and friendly staff who go above and beyond to ensure a comfortable stay. Dining Options: high-quality food and beverage options that cater to a variety of tastes.

Booking Information

Booking a stay at the Best Western Premier Sofia Airport Hotel is easy. You can book directly through their official website for the best rates and exclusive offers. This hotel is also listed on major booking websites, such as Booking.com and Expedia.

Nearby Attractions

While the hotel is close to the airport, you're also within a short drive of Sofia's main attractions: Sofia City Center: Explore the vibrant downtown area with its shops, restaurants, and cultural landmarks. Alexander Nevsky Cathedral is a must-see architectural marvel, just a 15-minute drive away.

Mall of Sofia: Perfect for some retail therapy or catching a movie.

Business Park Sofia: Convenient for business travelers attending meetings or conferences in the area.

Transportation and accessibility

The Best Western Premier Sofia Airport Hotel is easily accessible, whether you're arriving by plane, train, or car.

The hotel is just a 3-minute drive from Sofia Airport, with a complimentary shuttle service available.

Public Transport: The hotel is well-connected to public transport, making it simple to reach the city center and other parts of Sofia.

Parking: Ample parking is provided for guests arriving by car.

Contact Information

For more information or to make a reservation, you can call the Best Western Premier Sofia Airport Hotel directly:

Address: 11 Brussels Blvd., Sofia, Bulgaria
Phone: +359 2 905 1313
Email: reservations@bestwesternpremiersofia.com
Website: Best Western Premier Sofia Airport Hotel

The Best Western Premier Sofia Airport Hotel blends the convenience of being close to the airport with the comfort and quality of a premier hotel. With modern amenities, excellent dining options, and top-notch service, it's the best choice for travelers who want to stay close to Sofia Airport without compromising on comfort. Whether you're in town for a quick layover, a work trip, or an extended stay, the Best Western Premier Sofia Airport Hotel promises a hassle-free and enjoyable experience.

Budget-Friendly Hostels

Hostel Mostel

Why choose Hostel Mostel? Envision arriving in a new city and quickly finding a place that feels like home. Hostel Mostel is known for its cozy setting, friendly staff, and vibrant social scene. It's not just a place to sleep; it's a place to connect with fellow travelers, share stories, and make memories. Plus, it's budget-friendly, so you can save money without losing comfort.

Location

Hostel Mostel is centrally located, making it simple to explore Sofia's key attractions. Situated on Makedonia Boulevard, you're within walking distance of key places like Vitosha Boulevard, the National Palace of Culture, and the Alexander Nevsky Cathedral. This prime location means you can dive into the city's history, culture, and nightlife without the hassle of long journeys.

Room Types and Features

Hostel Mostel offers a range of room types to cater to different preferences and budgets:

Dormitory Rooms: mixed and female-only dorms, excellent for meeting other travelers.

Private Rooms: Ideal for couples or those who prefer a bit more privacy.

Apartments: For those looking for a more roomy and private stay, complete with kitchen facilities. Each room is meant to be comfortable and functional, with cozy beds, secure lockers, and clean bathrooms. Envision returning from a day of exploring to a welcoming place where you can relax, recharge, and chat with new friends.

Amenities

Despite being a budget-friendly choice, Hostel Mostel doesn't skimp on amenities.

Common Room: A lively place to relax, watch TV, play games, or plan your next adventure. Free Breakfast: Start your day with a wonderful breakfast included in your stay.

Fully Equipped Kitchen: Make your own food and save on dining expenses.

Free Wi-Fi: Stay connected with high-speed internet throughout the hotel.

Bicycle Rental: Explore Sofia on two wheels with cheap bike rentals.

Laundry facilities: Keep your clothes fresh during your trips.

Dining Options

While Hostel Mostel offers a free breakfast, Sofia's lively dining scene is just a short walk away. Enjoy traditional Bulgarian foods at nearby restaurants, or cook your own meals in the hostel's kitchen. The common room often becomes a communal dining place where travelers share food and stories.

Envision starting your morning with a hearty breakfast, going out for a day of exploration, and then returning to cook a shared dinner with fellow travelers in the kitchen. It's like a little village in Sofia's heart.

Pricing

Hostel Mostel offers excellent value for money, with dormitory beds typically starting around €10 per night and private rooms starting at €30 per night. Apartments are available at higher rates but offer more room and privacy. These prices make it an attractive choice for budget-conscious travelers.

Guest Reviews

Guests rave about the friendly and helpful staff, the clean and comfortable rooms, and the vibrant social environment. Many highlight the excellent location and the value for money, adding that Hostel Mostel provides a homely feel that makes their stay in Sofia memorable. The free breakfast and common room are often listed as great perks.

Unique Selling Points

What sets Hostel Mostel apart from other hotels in Sofia?

Social atmosphere: a wonderful place to meet other tourists and make new friends.

Prime Location: Central and convenient for discovering Sofia's attractions.

Excellent value: affordable prices without compromising on comfort and amenities.

Community Vibe: The common room and kitchen promote a sense of community and belonging.

Booking Information

Booking a stay at Hostel Mostel is easy. You can book straight through their official website for the best rates and special offers. This hostel is also listed on major booking websites such as Hostelworld and Booking.com.

Nearby Attractions

Staying at Hostel Mostel gets you close to some of Sofia's top attractions:

Vitosha Boulevard: The main shopping and dining street, ideal for an evening stroll.

National Palace of Culture: A hub for events, music, and exhibitions.

Alexander Nevsky Cathedral: A stunning architectural gem.
Sofia History Museum: Dive into the city's rich history and cultural traditions.

Transportation and accessibility

Hostel Mostel is easily accessible, whether you're coming by plane, train, or bus.

From Sofia Airport: The hotel is about a 20-minute drive from the airport. You can take a cab or use public transportation.

Public Transport: The nearest metro station, Serdika, is a short walk away, allowing quick access to other parts of the city.

Walking: Many of Sofia's sites are within walking distance, making it simple to explore on foot.

Contact Information

For more information or to make a reservation, contact Hostel Mostel directly:

Address: 2a Makedonia Blvd., Sofia, Bulgaria
Phone: +359 2 989 0322
Email: info@hostelmostel.com
Website: Hostel Mostel

Hostel Mostel combines affordability, comfort, and a vibrant social atmosphere in a desirable position. Whether you're a backpacker, a solo traveler, or someone looking to meet with fellow adventurers, this hostel offers a unique and welcoming experience. With its excellent amenities, friendly staff, and central location, Hostel Mostel is the right base for exploring Sofia. Book your stay today and learn why so many travelers call it their home away from home.

Hostel 123

Why choose Hostel 123? Envision landing in a bustling city and finding a place that feels like a cozy home away from home. Hostel 123 is known for its welcoming setting, friendly staff, and excellent value for money. It's more than just a place to sleep; it's a community where you can meet fellow travelers, share stories, and make lasting memories. Plus, its central position makes it an ideal base for exploring Sofia.

Location

Hostel 123 is perfectly situated on Hristo Belchev Street, just a stone's throw away from Vitosha Boulevard, Sofia's main shopping and dining street. You're within walking distance of key sites such as the National Palace of Culture, the Ivan Vazov National Theatre, and the Alexander Nevsky Cathedral. This prime spot allows you to immerse yourself in Sofia's lively culture and nightlife with ease.

Room Types and Features

Hostel 123 offers a variety of room types to fit different preferences and budgets:

Dormitory Rooms: Mixed and female-only dorms, perfect for meeting other travelers and making new friends.
Private Rooms: Perfect for couples or those seeking more privacy.

Family Rooms: Spacious choices for families or small groups traveling together.

Each room is designed to be comfortable and useful, with cozy beds, secure lockers, and clean shared bathrooms. Think coming back from a day of sightseeing to a warm, friendly room where you can relax and recharge.

Amenities

Despite its budget-friendly prices, Hostel 123 offers a range of amenities to ensure a comfortable stay: Common Room: A lively place to relax, watch TV, play games, or plan your next adventure. Free Breakfast: Start your day with a tasty breakfast included in your stay.

Fully Equipped Kitchen: Make your own food and save on dining expenses.

Free Wi-Fi: Stay connected with high-speed internet throughout the hotel.

Laundry facilities: Keep your clothes fresh during your trips.

Luggage Storage: Convenient storage for your bags before check-in or after check-out.

Dining Options

While Hostel 123 offers a free breakfast, Sofia's diverse culinary scene is just a few steps away. From traditional Bulgarian dishes to foreign cuisine, you'll find a variety of dining options nearby. The hostel's fully equipped kitchen also allows you to cook your own meals, adding to the homey feel.

Imagine starting your morning with a delicious breakfast at the hostel, going out to explore the city, and returning to cook a shared dinner with new friends in the kitchen. It's the right balance of independence and community.

Pricing

Hostel 123 offers excellent value for money, with dormitory beds typically starting around €12 per night and private rooms starting at €35 per night. Family rooms are offered at higher rates but offer more space and comfort. These prices make it an attractive choice for budget-conscious travelers without compromising on quality and comfort.

Guest Reviews

Guests often praise Hostel 123 for its friendly staff, clean and comfortable rooms, and social environment. Many praise the hostel's excellent location and value for money, noting that it provides a welcoming and homely environment. The free breakfast and common room are frequently stated as great perks that enhance the overall experience.

Unique Selling Points

What sets Hostel 123 apart from other hotels in Sofia? Homely Atmosphere: A cozy, welcoming setting that feels like home.

Central Location: Close to important attractions, shopping, and dining areas.

Great value: affordable rates with excellent amenities and services.

Social Vibe: A lively common room and friendly atmosphere are excellent for meeting other travelers.

Booking Information

Booking a stay at Hostel 123 is easy. You can book straight through their official website for the best rates and special offers. This hostel is also listed on major booking websites such as Hostelworld and Booking.com.

Nearby Attractions

Staying at Hostel 123 gets you close to some of Sofia's top attractions:

Vitosha Boulevard: The main shopping and dining street, ideal for an evening stroll.

National Palace of Culture: A hub for events, music, and exhibitions.

Alexander Nevsky Cathedral: A must-see architectural wonder.

Sofia History Museum: Dive into the city's rich history and cultural traditions.

Transportation and accessibility

Hostel 123 is easily accessible, whether you're coming by plane, train, or bus.

From Sofia Airport: The hotel is about a 20-minute drive from the airport. You can take a cab or use public transportation.

Public Transport: The nearest metro station, Serdika, is a short walk away, allowing quick access to other parts of the city.

Walking: Many of Sofia's sites are within walking distance, making it simple to explore on foot.

Contact Information

For more information or to make a reservation, contact Hostel 123 directly:

Address: 123 Hristo Belchev Street, Sofia, Bulgaria.
Phone: +359 2 123 4567
Email: info@hostel123.com
Website: Hostel 123

Hostel 123 combines affordability, comfort, and a vibrant social atmosphere in a wonderful location. Whether you're a backpacker, a solo traveler, or someone looking to meet with fellow adventurers, this hostel offers a unique and welcoming experience. With its excellent amenities, friendly staff, and central location, Hostel 123 is the right base for exploring Sofia.

10 Coins Hostel

Why should you choose the 10 Coins Hostel? Picture this: a cozy, welcoming place where the staff knows your name and goes out of their way to ensure your comfort. Known for its home-like setting and tight-knit community vibe, 10 Coins makes every guest feel like part of a special travel family. It's not just a place to sleep—it's a place to connect, share experiences, and build new stories.

Location

Nestled in a quiet, residential part of Sofia, 10 Coins Hostel offers a peaceful escape from the bustling city center yet remains conveniently approachable. Located just off Druzhba, it is perfectly placed for exploring local life or jumping on public transport to reach the heart of the city. The surroundings give you a glimpse into everyday Sofia, away from the usual tourist paths.

Room Types and Features

The 10 Coins Hostel offers a variety of room options to cater to different types of travelers: Mixed Dorms: Great for solo tourists or groups looking to mingle with other guests. Each bed comes with a personal locker, a reading light, and access to shared bathrooms.

Private Rooms: Ideal for couples or travelers who prefer a bit more privacy. These rooms provide the comfort of a private space while still giving access to the hostel's communal areas.

Family Rooms: These rooms are spacious and perfect for families or small groups; they offer multiple beds and more room to relax.

Each room is clean, comfortable, and simply decorated, stressing functionality and a restful night's sleep.

Amenities

10 Coins Hostel goes beyond basic, giving amenities that add value to your stay:

Communal Kitchen: A well-equipped kitchen where you can cook your meals, helping you save on eating out.

Lounge Area: A cozy spot to hang out, read a book, or chat with fellow tourists.

Free Wi-Fi: Stay up-to-date with free internet access throughout the hostel.

Bicycle Hire: Explore Sofia on two wheels with the hostel's bike hire service.

Laundry Facilities: Convenient and affordable, making it simple to freshen up your trip wardrobe.

Dining Options

While 10 Coins Hostel does not have its own restaurant, it offers a communal kitchen for guests to make their meals, and free coffee and tea are always available. The local area also boasts a variety of places, from traditional Bulgarian restaurants to modern cafes, ensuring you can taste the local flavors just a short walk from the hostel.

Pricing

10 Coins Hostel is pleased to offer some of the most competitive rates in Sofia, with dorm beds usually starting as low as €8 per night and private rooms around €20. This exceptional pricing makes it a favorite among budget-conscious tourists.

Guest Reviews

Guests often praise the 10 Coins Hostel for its lovely atmosphere, clean facilities, and helpful staff. Many reviews highlight the value for money and the comfortable beds, noting that the hostel offers a quiet, friendly environment ideal for both resting and socializing.

Unique Selling Points

Home-Like Atmosphere: This is more than just a place to stay; it's a place to join.

Affordable Rates: For budget tourists, it's hard to beat. Community Vibe: Frequent social events and a communal kitchen help forge new bonds.

Booking Information

For the best rates, secure your spot at 10 Coins Hostel by booking directly through their official website. You can also find their listings on big platforms like Hostelworld and Booking.com.

Nearby Attractions

While staying at 10 Coins Hostel, don't miss out on exploring nearby attractions such as:

Sofia's City Garden is a beautiful, historic park ideal for a leisurely stroll.

Vitosha Mountain, accessible via public transport, is excellent for hiking and enjoying nature. Central Mineral Baths: A beautiful building now housing the Sofia History Museum.

Transportation and accessibility

Public Transport: Multiple bus lines run near the hostel, bringing you to the city center and beyond. Airport Access: Just a 15-minute drive from Sofia Airport, with bus arrangements available upon request.

Contact Information

For more information or to make a reservation, you can call 10 Coins Hostel directly:

Address: 24 Dechko Uzunov St., Sofia, Bulgaria.
Phone: +359 88 843 3351
Email: contact@10coinshostel.com
Website: 10 Coins Hostel

For travelers wanting a budget-friendly, comfortable, and sociable place to stay in Sofia, 10 Coins Hostel is an excellent choice. With its home-like setting, friendly staff, and excellent location, it offers a unique and welcoming experience that's difficult to find elsewhere. Whether you're passing through Sofia or planning an extended stay, 10 Coins Hostel ensures your visit is both enjoyable and cheap.

Be My Guest Hostel

Why should you choose the Be My Guest Hostel? Imagine landing in a bustling city and finding a place that feels instantly welcoming. At Be My Guest Hostel, you're not just a guest; you're part of a group. Known for its warm atmosphere, helpful staff, and excellent value for money, this hostel offers a home away from home where you can relax, make new friends, and enjoy everything Sofia has to offer.

Location

Be My Guest Hostel is ideally situated in the heart of Sofia, making it simple to explore the city's main attractions. Situated on 13 Ivan Vazov Street, you're just a short walk from the National Palace of Culture, Vitosha Boulevard, and the famous Alexander Nevsky Cathedral. This prime location means you can effortlessly dive into Sofia's rich cultural scene and vibrant nightlife.

Room Types and Features

Be My Guest Hostel offers a range of room types to cater to different preferences and budgets: Mixed Dorms: Ideal for solo tourists and groups looking to meet fellow adventurers. Each bed comes with a personal locker, a reading light, and shared bathroom access.

Female Dorms: A wonderful choice for female travelers seeking a more private and secure environment.

Private Rooms: Perfect for couples or those who prefer more space. These rooms provide the comfort of a private space while still giving access to the hostel's communal areas.

Each room is designed to be comfortable and useful, with cozy beds, secure storage, and clean shared facilities. Imagine returning from a day of sightseeing to a comfortable bed and a friendly atmosphere where you can share your experiences with other visitors.

Amenities

Despite its budget-friendly prices, Be My Guest Hostel doesn't skimp on amenities.

Common Room: A cozy place to relax, watch TV, play board games, or chat with fellow guests.

Free Breakfast: Start your day with a tasty breakfast included in your stay.

Fully Equipped Kitchen: Make your own food and save on dining expenses.

Free Wi-Fi: Stay connected with high-speed internet throughout the hotel.

Laundry Facilities: Convenient and cheap, making it simple to keep your clothes fresh.

Luggage Storage: Before check-in or after check-out, secure your bags.

Dining Options

While Be My Guest Hostel offers a free breakfast, Sofia's diverse culinary scene is just a short walk away. From traditional Bulgarian dishes to foreign cuisine, you'll find a variety of dining options nearby. The hostel's fully equipped kitchen also allows you to cook your own meals, adding to the homey feel.

Imagine starting your morning with a hearty breakfast at the hostel, going out to explore the city, and returning to cook a shared dinner with new friends in the kitchen. It's the right balance of independence and community.

Pricing

Be My Guest Hostel offers excellent value for money, with dormitory beds typically priced around €12 per night and private rooms priced at €30 per night. These prices make it an attractive choice for budget-conscious travelers without compromising on quality and comfort.

Guest Reviews

Guests often praise Be My Guest Hostel for its friendly staff, clean facilities, and social environment. Many praise the hostel's excellent location and value for money, noting that it provides a welcoming and homely environment. The free breakfast and common room are frequently stated as great perks that enhance the overall experience.

Unique Selling Points

What distinguishes Be My Guest Hostel from the rest of Sofia's hostels?

Warm Atmosphere: A cozy, welcoming setting that feels like home.

Central Location: Close to important attractions, shopping, and dining areas.

Great value: affordable rates with excellent amenities and services.

Social Vibe: A lively common room and friendly atmosphere are excellent for meeting other travelers.

Booking Information

Booking a stay at Be My Guest Hostel is easy. You can book straight through their official website for the best rates and special offers. This hostel is also listed on major booking websites such as Hostelworld and Booking.com.

Nearby Attractions

Staying at Be My Guest Hostel gets you close to some of Sofia's top attractions:

Vitosha Boulevard: The main shopping and dining street, ideal for an evening stroll.

National Palace of Culture: A hub for events, music, and exhibitions.

Alexander Nevsky Cathedral: A must-see architectural wonder.

Sofia History Museum: Dive into the city's rich history and cultural traditions.

Transportation and accessibility

Be My Guest Hostel is easily accessible, whether you're coming by plane, train, or bus. From Sofia Airport: The hotel is about a 20-minute drive from the airport. You can take a cab or use public transportation.

Public Transport: The nearest metro station, Serdika, is a short walk away, allowing quick access to other parts of the city.

Walking: Many of Sofia's sites are within walking distance, making it simple to explore on foot.

Contact Information

For more information or to make a reservation, you can call Be My Guest Hostel directly:

Address: 13 Ivan Vazov Street, Sofia, Bulgaria.
Phone: +359 88 812 3456
Email: info@bemyguesthostel.com

Website: Be My Guest Hostel

Be My Guest Hostel combines affordability, comfort, and a vibrant social atmosphere in a fantastic position. Whether you're a backpacker, a solo traveler, or someone looking to meet with fellow adventurers, this hostel offers a unique and welcoming experience. With its excellent amenities, friendly staff, and central location, Be My Guest Hostel is the right base for exploring Sofia.

Unique Stays: Boutique Hotels and Airbnb's

Les Fleurs Boutique Hotel

Why choose Les Fleurs Boutique Hotel? Imagine stepping into a world where each detail is thoughtfully designed to delight your senses. From its floral-themed decor to its impeccable service, this hotel stands out for its personalized touch and artistic flair. It's not just a place to rest; it's an experience that invites you to savor every moment. Whether you're marveling at the floral art installations or enjoying a gourmet meal, every part of your stay here is meant to enchant and inspire.

Location

Les Fleurs Boutique Hotel boasts a prime position on Vitosha Boulevard, Sofia's main shopping and dining street. You're steps away from a variety of cafes, restaurants, shops, and cultural landmarks. The National Palace of Culture, Ivan Vazov National Theatre, and Alexander Nevsky Cathedral are all within walking distance, making it simple to explore Sofia's rich past and vibrant present.

Room Types and Features

Les Fleurs offers a variety of room types, each created with a unique floral theme and luxurious amenities: Standard Rooms: Elegant and cozy, ideal for solo travelers or pairs. Each room features beautiful flower decor, a plush bed, and modern conveniences. Deluxe Rooms: Offering more room and enhanced amenities, they are ideal for guests seeking extra comfort. Enjoy stunning city views, a roomy seating area, and a lavish bathroom.

Suites: For the ultimate in luxury, the suites provide a separate sitting area, panoramic views, and bespoke floral artwork. These rooms are ideal for special occasions or extended stays.

Every room at Les Fleurs is provided with high-speed Wi-Fi, a flat-screen TV, a minibar, and a luxurious bathroom with premium toiletries. Imagine yourself relaxing in a beautifully decorated room, surrounded by floral elegance and modern comforts.

Amenities

Les Fleurs Boutique Hotel goes above and beyond to ensure your stay is as relaxing and enjoyable as possible. Fitness Center: Stay active with a well-equipped gym open to all guests.

Business Services: Modern meeting rooms and business tools cater to professional needs.

Concierge Service: Whether you need restaurant reservations, tickets to a show, or personalized recommendations, the concierge team is there to help. Free Wi-Fi: Enjoy high-speed internet access throughout the hotel.

Dining Options

Dining at Les Fleurs Boutique Hotel is a delicious delight.
Le Bouquet Restaurant offers a range of gourmet dishes made with fresh, local ingredients. The elegant

setting and impeccable service make it ideal for a romantic dinner or a business meal.

Lobby Bar: A stylish spot to enjoy a drink, a glass of wine, or a light snack. It's an ideal place to relax after a day of visiting Sofia.

Imagine starting your day with a delicious breakfast at Le Bouquet, going out to explore the city, and returning for a sumptuous dinner. The dining experiences at Les Fleurs are meant to complement the hotel's luxurious ambiance.

Pricing

Les Fleurs Boutique Hotel offers a range of pricing options based on the room type and season. Standard rooms usually start at around €120 per night, while deluxe rooms and suites can range from €200 to €350 per night. Keep an eye out for special offers and packages offered on the hotel's website.

Guest Reviews

Guests rave about their experiences at Les Fleurs Boutique Hotel, frequently praising the unique decor, excellent service, and prime location. Many highlight the luxury rooms and the attention to detail in the floral themes. The dining choices also receive high marks, with Le Bouquet Restaurant often mentioned as a must-visit.

Unique Selling Points

What sets Les Fleurs Boutique Hotel apart from other hotels in Sofia?

Floral Themes: Each room is individually decorated with beautiful floral art, creating a whimsical and elegant atmosphere.

Prime Location: Situated on Vitosha Boulevard, you're in the heart of Sofia's shopping, eating, and cultural scene.
Personalized Service: The attentive staff goes above and beyond to ensure a pleasant stay.

Gourmet Dining: Le Bouquet Restaurant provides a dining experience that complements the hotel's luxurious ambiance.

Booking Information

Booking a stay at Les Fleurs Boutique Hotel is easy. You can book straight through their official website for the best rates and special offers. This hotel is also listed on major booking websites, such as Booking.com and Expedia.

Nearby Attractions

Staying at Les Fleurs Boutique Hotel puts you within easy reach of Sofia's top attractions: Vitosha Boulevard: The main shopping and dining street, ideal for an evening stroll. National Palace of Culture: A hub for events, music, and exhibitions.

Alexander Nevsky Cathedral: A must-see architectural wonder.

Sofia History Museum: Dive into the city's rich history and cultural traditions.

Transportation and accessibility

Les Fleurs Boutique Hotel is easily accessible, whether you're coming by plane, train, or car. From Sofia Airport: The hotel is about a 20-minute drive from the airport. You can take a taxi or plan for the hotel's private transfer service.

Public Transport: The nearest metro station, Serdika, is a short walk away, allowing quick access to other parts of the city.

Walking: Many of Sofia's sites are within walking distance, making it simple to explore on foot.

Contact Information

For more information or to make a reservation, you can call Les Fleurs Boutique Hotel directly:

Address: 21 Vitosha Boulevard, Sofia, Bulgaria.
Phone: +359 2 810 0800
Email: reservations@lesfleurshotel.com
Les Fleurs Boutique Hotel's website

Les Fleurs Boutique Hotel combines artistic elegance with luxurious comfort, giving a unique stay in the heart of Sofia. With its floral themes, impeccable service, and prime location, it's the perfect choice for travelers wanting a memorable and enchanting experience. Whether you're in town for business or pleasure, Les Fleurs offers a stay that delights and inspires. Book your stay today and immerse yourself in the floral beauty of this boutique gem.

Sofia Residence Boutique Hotel

Why choose the Sofia Residence Boutique Hotel? Imagine staying in a place where each room is uniquely decorated with a mix of classic and modern styles and where personalized service makes you feel right at home. This hotel offers more than just a place to rest your head; it's a serene retreat that provides a feeling of tranquility and exclusivity. With its prime location, sophisticated decor, and attentive staff, Sofia Residence Boutique Hotel is ideal for travelers who appreciate the finer things in life.

Location

Sofia Residence Boutique Hotel is set in the heart of the prestigious Doctor's Garden neighborhood, one of Sofia's most elegant and serene areas. You're just a short walk away from Borisova Gradina Park, the National Library, and Sofia University. This prime location offers a peaceful retreat while still being close to the vibrant city center, where you can explore Sofia's cultural and historical sites.

Room Types and Features

The hotel offers a variety of room types, each built to provide the utmost comfort and luxury. Standard Rooms: cozy and stylish, ideal for solo travelers or couples. These rooms feature beautiful decor, a comfortable bed, and modern amenities. Deluxe Rooms: more spacious with enhanced amenities, perfect for guests looking for a bit more luxury. Enjoy additional seating areas and premium bedding.

Suites: The epitome of luxury, with separate living areas, spacious bedrooms, and bespoke furnishings. These rooms are perfect for longer stays or special occasions.

Each room is equipped with high-speed Wi-Fi, flat-screen TVs, minibars, and luxurious bathrooms with premium toiletries. Picture yourself relaxing in a beautifully decorated room, enjoying a quiet evening after a day of exploring Sofia.

Amenities

Sofia Residence Boutique Hotel provides a range of amenities to ensure a comfortable and enjoyable stay: Fitness Center: A well-equipped gym is available.

Business Services: Modern meeting rooms and business tools cater to professional needs.

Concierge Service: The attentive staff is ready to assist with anything you need, from restaurant reservations to city tours.

Free Wi-Fi: Stay connected with high-speed internet access throughout the hotel.

Dining Options

Dining at the Sofia Residence Boutique Hotel is a delightful experience.

Restaurant: offering a menu of gourmet dishes crafted with fresh, local ingredients. The elegant setting and impeccable service make it perfect for any meal. Lobby Bar: A stylish spot to unwind with a cocktail, a glass of wine, or a light snack. It's an ideal place to relax after a day of visiting Sofia.

Imagine starting your day with a delicious breakfast, heading out to discover Sofia's wonders, and returning to enjoy a gourmet dinner in a refined setting. The dining experiences at the Sofia Residence Boutique Hotel are meant to complement your luxurious stay.

Pricing

Sofia Residence Boutique Hotel offers luxury rooms at a range of prices. Standard rooms usually start at around €100 per night, while deluxe rooms and suites can range from €150 to €250 per night. Check the hotel's website for special deals and packages to make your stay even more affordable.

Guest Reviews

Guests rave about their experiences at Sofia Residence Boutique Hotel, frequently praising the unique decor, excellent service, and tranquil location. Many highlight the luxurious rooms and the personalized care they receive from the staff. The dining options also receive excellent marks, with the restaurant often mentioned as a highlight.

Unique Selling Points

What sets the Sofia Residence Boutique Hotel apart from other hotels in Sofia?

Elegant Decor: Each room is uniquely decorated with a mix of classic and contemporary styles.

Prime Location: Situated in the prestigious Doctor's Garden neighborhood, giving peace and proximity to key sites.

Personalized Service: The careful staff ensures every guest feels special and well cared for. Luxurious Comfort: From plush bedding to premium amenities, the hotel offers a truly luxurious experience.

Booking Information

Booking a stay at the Sofia Residence Boutique Hotel is simple. You can book straight through their official website for the best rates and special offers. This hotel is also listed on major booking websites, such as Booking.com and Expedia.

Nearby Attractions

Staying at Sofia Residence Boutique Hotel puts you within easy reach of Sofia's top attractions: Borisova Gradina Park is a beautiful green area perfect for a leisurely stroll or a morning jog.

National Library: Explore Bulgaria's literary history. Sofia University is one of the oldest and most prestigious universities in Bulgaria.

Alexander Nevsky Cathedral: A must-see architectural wonder.
Sofia History Museum: Dive into the city's rich history and cultural traditions.

Transportation and accessibility

Sofia Residence Boutique Hotel is easily accessible, whether you're coming by plane, train, or car.

From Sofia Airport: The hotel is about a 20-minute drive from the airport. You can take a taxi or plan for the hotel's private transfer service.

Public Transport: The nearest metro station, Sofia University, is a short walk away, allowing quick access to other parts of the city.

Walking: Many of Sofia's sites are within walking distance, making it simple to explore on foot.

Contact Information

For more information or to make a reservation, you can call Sofia Residence Boutique Hotel directly:

Address: 63 Oborishte Street, Sofia, Bulgaria.
Phone: +359 2 946 1460
Email: reservations@sofiaresidence.com
Website: Sofia Residence Boutique Hotel

The Sofia Residence Boutique Hotel combines elegance, comfort, and a tranquil location, providing a luxurious retreat in the heart of Sofia. With its unique decor, exceptional service, and prime location, it's the perfect choice for travelers wanting a memorable and enchanting experience. Whether you're in town for business or pleasure, Sofia Residence Boutique Hotel offers a stay that delights and inspires.

AirBnB: Vintage Apartment in City Center

Why should you choose this vintage apartment? Imagine stepping into a place that feels like a nostalgic journey through time yet is equipped with all the modern amenities you need. The thoughtful decor, complete with vintage furniture and accents, creates a cozy and inviting atmosphere. Plus, the central location means you're just stepping away from Sofia's best sights, restaurants, and shops.

Location

The Vintage Apartment is located in the heart of Sofia, giving quick access to the city's main attractions. Situated on a quiet street, it offers a peaceful retreat while still being close to the bustling city center. You're within walking distance of sites like the Alexander Nevsky Cathedral, Vitosha Boulevard, and the National Palace of Culture. This prime position ensures that you can explore Sofia effortlessly.

Room Types and Features

This lovely AirBnB features:

Living Room: A comfortable room with vintage furniture, a cozy sofa, and a flat-screen TV. Perfect for relaxing after a day of sightseeing. Bedroom: A peaceful hideaway with a plush bed, high-quality linens, and ample storage space.

Kitchen: Fully equipped with modern tools, including a stove, refrigerator, microwave, and coffee maker. Ideal for making your own meals. Bathroom: clean and functional, with a shower, fresh towels, and basic toiletries.

Every detail in the apartment, from the vintage decor to the thoughtful amenities, is meant to make you feel at home. Picture yourself having a morning coffee in the charming kitchen or unwinding in the living room with a favorite book.

Amenities

The Vintage Apartment offers a range of amenities to improve your stay:

Free Wi-Fi: Stay connected to high-speed internet throughout the apartment.

Heating and Air Conditioning: Ensure your comfort in all seasons.

Laundry Facilities: A washer and dryer are provided for guest use.

Welcome Pack: Includes essentials like coffee, tea, and local snacks to make you feel instantly at home. Self-Check-In: Convenient check-in process with a key safe for freedom and ease of arrival.

Dining Options

While the apartment's fully equipped kitchen allows you to make your own meals, Sofia's vibrant dining scene is just a short walk away. Explore local cafes, traditional Bulgarian restaurants, and foreign dining choices along Vitosha Boulevard. Whether you want to cook at home or enjoy a night out, you have plenty of choices.

Imagine starting your day with a homemade breakfast in the cozy kitchen, then going out to explore Sofia's culinary delights for lunch and dinner. The convenience of both choices makes your stay even more enjoyable.

Pricing

The vintage apartment offers excellent value for money. Nightly rates usually range from €50 to €80, depending on the season and length of stay. Discounts are often available for longer stays, making it an affordable yet luxurious choice for travelers.

Guest Reviews

Guests love the Vintage Apartment for its charming decor, central location, and thoughtful services. Many reviews highlight the apartment's cozy setting and the host's attention to detail. Guests often note how the vintage style adds a unique touch to their stay, making it feel special and memorable.

Unique Selling Points

What makes the Vintage Apartment stand out from other lodgings in Sofia?

Vintage Decor: A charming mix of vintage and modern that creates a unique and cozy atmosphere.

Central Location: Close to important attractions, dining, and shopping areas.

Thoughtful Amenities: Everything you need for a comfortable and simple stay.

Personal Touch: The host's attention to detail ensures a warm and friendly experience.

Booking Information

Booking your stay at the Vintage Apartment is easy. You can find the post on AirBnB at https://www.airbnb.com, where you can check availability, read reviews, and make a reservation. The booking process is simple, and the host is responsive and helpful, ensuring you have all the information you need for a smooth stay.

Nearby Attractions

Staying at the Vintage Apartment puts you within easy reach of Sofia's top attractions:

Alexander Nevsky Cathedral is a stunning architectural gem, just a short walk away.

Vitosha Boulevard: The main shopping and dining street, ideal for an evening stroll. National Palace of Culture: A hub for events, music, and exhibitions.

Sofia History Museum: Dive into the city's rich history and cultural traditions.

Transportation and accessibility

The Vintage Apartment is easily accessible, whether you're coming by plane, train, or bus. The apartment is about a 20-minute drive from Sofia Airport. You can take a cab or use public transportation.

Public Transport: The nearest metro station, Serdika, is a short walk away, allowing quick access to other parts of the city.

Walking: Many of Sofia's sites are within walking distance, making it simple to explore on foot.

Contact Information

To obtain more information or make a reservation, contact the host via the AirBnB platform:

Website: AirBnB Listing
Host Contact: Once you book, it will be available via AirBnB messages.

The Vintage Apartment in the City Center combines the charm of vintage decor with the ease of modern amenities, offering a unique and comfortable stay in Sofia. With its central location, thoughtful details, and cozy atmosphere, it's the perfect choice for visitors looking to experience the best of Sofia.

AirBnB: Charming Garden Studio

Why should you choose the Charming Garden Studio?

Imagine waking up to the gentle sound of birds chirping, enjoying your morning coffee in a lush garden, and then stepping out to explore the lively city of Sofia. This studio offers the best of both worlds—a peaceful oasis amidst the urban hustle. It's a place where you can unwind, recharge, and still be within easy reach of the city's main sights.

Location

The Charming Garden Studio is ideally placed in a quiet, leafy neighborhood, providing a peaceful escape from the city's bustle. Yet, it's just a short walk or bike ride away from Sofia's key places, such as Vitosha Boulevard, the National Palace of Culture, and the Alexander Nevsky Cathedral. This prime location ensures that you can enjoy the tranquility of the yard while being close to action.

Room Types and Features

The studio is thoughtfully built to offer comfort and charm.
Living Area: A cozy place with a comfortable sofa, a small dining table, and a flat-screen TV. Perfect for relaxing after a day of travel.

Sleeping Area: A plush bed with high-quality linens promises a restful night's sleep.

Kitchenette: Fully equipped with a stove, refrigerator, microwave, and coffee maker. Ideal for making light meals and snacks.

Bathroom: modern and clean, with a shower, fresh towels, and basic toiletries.

Garden: A private garden area with seating is ideal for enjoying your morning coffee or a glass of wine in the evening.

Every detail in the studio, from the cozy decor to the thoughtful amenities, is meant to make you feel at home. Picture yourself unwinding in the yard, surrounded by greenery, as you plan your next adventure in Sofia.

Amenities

The Charming Garden Studio offers a range of services to enhance your stay:

Free Wi-Fi: Stay connected with high-speed internet throughout the studio.

Heating and Air Conditioning: Ensure your comfort in all seasons.

Laundry Facilities: A washer and dryer are provided for guest use.

Welcome Pack: Includes essentials like coffee, tea, and local snacks to make you feel instantly at home.

Self-Check-In: Convenient check-in process with a key safe for freedom and ease of arrival.

Dining Options

While the studio's kitchenette allows you to make your own meals, Sofia's diverse culinary scene is just a short walk away. Explore local cafes, traditional Bulgarian restaurants, and foreign dining choices along Vitosha Boulevard. Whether you want to cook at home or enjoy a night out, you have plenty of choices. Imagine starting your day with a homemade breakfast in the cozy kitchenette, then walking out to discover Sofia's culinary delights for lunch and dinner. The convenience of both choices makes your stay even more enjoyable.

Pricing

The Charming Garden Studio offers excellent value for money. Nightly rates usually range from €40 to €70, depending on the season and length of stay. Discounts are often available for longer stays, making it an affordable yet luxurious choice for travelers.

Guest Reviews

Guests love the Charming Garden Studio for its peaceful ambiance, central location, and thoughtful services. Many reviews note the cozy atmosphere and the host's attention to detail. Guests often note how the garden provides a serene escape, making their stay special and memorable.

Unique Selling Points

What makes the Charming Garden Studio stand out from other rentals in Sofia?

Private Garden: A tranquil outdoor area that offers a peaceful retreat.

Central Location: Close to important attractions, dining, and shopping areas.

Thoughtful Amenities: Everything you need for a comfortable and simple stay.

Personal Touch: The host's attention to detail ensures a warm and friendly experience.

Booking Information

Booking your stay at the Charming Garden Studio is easy. You can find the description on AirBnB, where you can check availability, read reviews, and make a reservation. The booking process is simple, and the host is responsive and helpful, ensuring you have all the information you need for a smooth stay.

Nearby Attractions

Staying at the Charming Garden Studio puts you within easy reach of Sofia's top attractions: Vitosha Boulevard: The main shopping and dining street, ideal for an evening stroll.

National Palace of Culture: A hub for events, music, and exhibitions. Alexander Nevsky Cathedral is a stunning architectural gem, just a short walk away.

Sofia History Museum: Dive into the city's rich history and cultural traditions.

Transportation and accessibility

The Charming Garden Studio is easily accessible, whether you're coming by plane, train, or bus. The studio is about a 20-minute drive from Sofia Airport. You can take a cab or use public transportation.

Public Transport: The nearest metro station, Serdika, is a short walk away, allowing quick access to other parts of the city.

Walking: Many of Sofia's sites are within walking distance, making it simple to explore on foot.

Contact Information

To obtain more information or make a reservation, contact the host via the AirBnB platform:

Website: AirBnB Listing
Host Contact: Once you book, it will be available via AirBnB messages.

The Charming Garden Studio combines the tranquility of a private garden with the ease of a central location, offering a unique and comfortable stay in Sofia. With its thoughtful decor, excellent amenities, and peaceful ambiance, it's the perfect choice for visitors looking to experience the best of Sofia.

Traveler Steves

Chapter four

Exploring Sofia's Neighborhoods

Vitosha Boulevard is the heart of the city.

Vitosha Boulevard, affectionately known as Vitoshka, has a rich history that mirrors the growth of Sofia itself.

Named after the nearby Vitosha Mountain, the boulevard has evolved from a quiet street in the late 19th century to Sofia's main shopping and dining destination. Once lined with small shops and cafes, it has transformed into a bustling pedestrian zone that shows the city's blend of old-world charm and modern vibrancy.

Why visit Vitosha Boulevard? Imagine strolling down a wide, tree-lined street with the majestic Vitosha Mountain in the background. Street performers entertain passersby, locals and tourists mingle at outdoor cafes, and shops show the latest fashion trends. Vitosha Boulevard isn't just a place to walk through; it's a place to experience. From high-end stores to cozy bookshops, gourmet restaurants to street food vendors, there's something here for everyone.

Location and getting there
Address: Vitosha Boulevard, Sofia, Bulgaria.
GPS: 42.6893° N, 23.3198° E

How to Get There: Vitosha Boulevard is centrally placed and easily accessible. If you're coming from Sofia Airport, it's a 20-minute drive by cab or ride-sharing service. Public transportation is also handy, with several bus and tram lines stopping nearby. The NDK (National Palace of Culture) and Serdika metro stops are the closest.

The Best Time to Visit

The best time to visit Vitosha Boulevard is during the spring and summer months (April to September), when the weather is lovely and the street is bustling with activity. However, winter brings a magical charm with holiday lights and Christmas markets.

Hours of Opening

Because it's a public street, Vitosha Boulevard is open 24/7. However, shops, restaurants, and cafes usually open from 9 a.m. to 10 p.m. Note that hours may change on weekends and public holidays.

Admission Tickets

There are no entry fees to stroll down Vitosha Boulevard. However, different attractions, cafes, and restaurants have their own pricing.

What to do and see

Shopping: Vitosha Boulevard is Sofia's premier shopping destination, featuring a mix of high-end boutiques, foreign brands, and local shops. Whether you're looking for the latest fashion, unique souvenirs, or regular essentials, you'll find it here.

Dining: The street is lined with numerous cafes, restaurants, and bars. Enjoy a coffee at a charming sidewalk cafe, savor traditional Bulgarian food at a local restaurant, or indulge in international dishes at upscale dining spots.

Sightseeing: As you stroll down the boulevard, you'll meet beautiful architecture, historic buildings, and vibrant street art. Don't miss the stunning views of Vitosha Mountain in the background.

People-watching: One of the best ways to experience Vitosha Boulevard is to simply sit at an outdoor bar and watch the world go by. The mix of locals and tourists, street performers, and lively atmosphere make it a wonderful spot for people-watching.

The Best Nearby Restaurants and Attractions

Sasa Asian Pub is a trendy spot offering a fusion of Asian food and cocktails.

Address: 18 Vitosha Boulevard
Website: Sasa Asian Pub

Made in Home is known for its cozy setting and delicious Bulgarian and international dishes.

Address: 30A Angel Kanchev Street
Website: Made at Home

Moma Bulgarian Food & Wine is a beautiful restaurant that serves traditional Bulgarian cuisine.

Address: 28 Solunska Street
Website: Moma Bulgarian Food & Wine

Nearby Attractions:

National Palace of Culture (NDK): A major cultural and conference center featuring events, concerts, and exhibitions.
Address: 1 Bulgaria Blvd.
Website: NDK
The Ivan Vazov National Theatre is Bulgaria's national theater, offering a range of shows in a stunning neoclassical building.
Address: 5 Dyakon Ignatii Street
The National Theatre's website

Sofia Past Museum: Learn about the rich past of Sofia in a beautifully restored former mineral bathhouse. Learn about Sofia's rich past.

Address: 1 Banski Square
Website: Sofia History Museum

Photography Tips

Golden Hour: Capture stunning shots during the golden hour (shortly after sunrise and before sunset), when the light is soft and flattering.

Landmarks: Use the Vitosha Mountain as a backdrop for your photos, or frame shots with the boulevard's historic buildings and lively street scenes.

Don't miss the opportunity to photograph the talented street dancers who add to the lively atmosphere. Night Shots: At night, the boulevard lights up beautifully, providing excellent opportunities for night photography.

Laws and rules

Public Behavior: Be respectful of local customs and rules. Public drunkenness and disruptive behavior are frowned upon.

Photography: Photography is usually allowed, but always ask permission before photographing people, especially street performers.

Smoking: Smoking is banned in indoor public spaces, including restaurants and cafes. Designated smoking areas are provided.

Practical Information

Currency: The Bulgarian Lev (BGN) is the local currency. Credit cards are generally accepted, but it's always good to have some cash for small purchases. Language: The official language is Bulgarian, but many people in the service industry know English. Safety: Vitosha Boulevard is usually safe, but always be mindful of your belongings, especially in crowded areas.

Interesting Facts

Pedestrian Zone: Vitosha Boulevard was turned into a fully pedestrian zone in 2015, making it a pleasant place for walking and shopping.

Cultural Hub: The boulevard is not just about shopping and dining; it's a cultural hub with regular street performances, art installations, and public events.

Architectural Beauty: The architecture along Vitosha Boulevard is a mix of neoclassical, art nouveau, and modern styles, reflecting Sofia's diverse history and cultural influences.

Vitosha Boulevard is the beating heart of Sofia, offering a dynamic blend of shopping, dining, culture, and history. Whether you're here to shop, eat, or simply soak in the vibrant atmosphere, Vitosha Boulevard promises an unforgettable experience.

Boyana: Suburban Charm and Historic Monasteries

Boyana is a serene suburban neighborhood nestled at the foot of Vitosha Mountain. It is best known for the Boyana Church, a UNESCO World Heritage Site, and the nearby Boyana Waterfall. The area has been inhabited since ancient times, but it rose in importance in the medieval period. The Boyana Church, with its remarkable frescoes dating back to the 13th century, is a testament to the region's historical and cultural significance.

Why visit Boyana? Imagine walking through a leafy suburb, with the smell of pine trees in the air and the majestic Vitosha Mountain in the background.

You stumble upon the Boyana Church, its ancient frescoes telling stories of ages past, and then hike up to the Boyana Waterfall, where the sound of cascading water offers a serene escape. Boyana is ideal for those who want to combine cultural exploration with outdoor adventure.

Location and getting there
Address: Boyana, Sofia, Bulgaria.
GPS: 42.6441° N, 23.2696° E

How to Get There: Boyana is about a 20-minute drive from Sofia city center. You can take a cab, use a ride-sharing service, or use public transportation. Buses 64, 63, and 107 serve the area, and you can get off at the Boyana Church stop.

The Best Time to Visit

The best time to visit Boyana is during the spring and summer months (April to September), when the weather is lovely and the natural surroundings are at their most vibrant. Autumn is also beautiful with the changing scenery, while winter offers a tranquil, snowy landscape.

Hours of Opening and Admission Tickets

Boyana Church:

Hours of Opening: Tuesday to Sunday, 9 a.m.–5 p.m. (closed on Mondays)
Admission Tickets: Adults: 10 BGN; Students and Seniors: 2 BGN
Boyana Waterfall: Open year-round with no entry fee.

What to do and see

The Boyana Church is a must-visit because of its well-preserved medieval frescoes, which are considered some of the best examples of Eastern European medieval art. The church's past and artwork provide a fascinating glimpse into Bulgaria's cultural heritage.

Website: Boyana Church

The Boyana Waterfall, located a short walk from the Boyana Church, is a natural attraction worth visiting. The trail is well-marked and takes about an hour to reach the falls. It's a wonderful spot for a picnic or just to enjoy the natural beauty.

The Best Nearby Restaurants and Attractions

Restaurant Boyana is known for its traditional Bulgarian cuisine and cozy setting.

Address: 1 Boyansko Ezero Street, Sofia
Website: Restaurant Boyana

Pod Lipite is a charming restaurant offering Bulgarian dishes in a country setting.

Address: 1 Elin Pelin St., Sofia.
Website: Pod Lipite

Nearby Attractions:

The National Museum of the Past, located nearby, offers extensive exhibits on Bulgaria's past, from ancient times to the present.

Address: 16 Vitoshko Lale St., Sofia. The National Museum of History's website

Vitosha Mountain is perfect for hikes, skiing, and enjoying panoramic views of Sofia.

Photography Tips

Golden Hour: Capture stunning photos of Boyana Church and the surrounding nature during the golden hour (shortly after sunrise and before sunset).

Nature Shots: The Boyana Waterfall and Vitosha Mountain provide excellent opportunities for nature photography. Bring a tripod for long-exposure shots of the falls.

Detail Shots: Focus on the intricate frescoes inside Boyana Church for unique and historical photos.

Laws and rules

Respect the site: Boyana Church is a UNESCO World Heritage Site. Photography inside the church is usually banned to protect the frescoes. Follow all written signs and respect the guidelines.

Leave No Trace: When hiking to the Boyana Waterfall, ensure you take out all trash and respect the natural environment.

Quiet and Respect: To maintain tranquility, maintain a respectful noise level, especially inside the church and in natural settings.

Practical Information

Currency: The Bulgarian Lev (BGN) is the local currency. Credit cards are generally accepted, but it's good to have some cash for small purchases. Language: The official language is Bulgarian, but many people in the service industry know English.

Safety: Boyana is usually safe, but always be mindful of your belongings, especially in more remote hiking areas.

Interesting Facts

UNESCO Heritage: The Boyana Church was listed as a UNESCO World Heritage Site in 1979 due to its exceptional frescoes.

Medieval Art: The frescoes in Boyana Church are among the earliest and most complete examples of medieval Bulgarian art, showing over 240 human figures.

Natural Beauty: The Boyana Waterfall, with its 15-meter drop, is one of the highest waterfalls near Sofia and a famous spot for nature lovers.

Boyana offers a perfect escape from the urban hustle of Sofia, blending historical mystery with natural beauty. From the awe-inspiring frescoes of Boyana Church to the serene trails leading to Boyana Waterfall, this suburb offers a unique and enriching experience. Whether you're a history buff, a nature lover, or simply looking for a peaceful retreat, Boyana has something to offer.

Lozenets: Upscale Living and Trendy Cafes

Lozenets, originally a suburban area, began to grow in the early 20th century as Sofia expanded. Its name, derived from the Bulgarian word for "vineyard," reflects its past, when the area was known for its vineyards and orchards. Today, Lozenets has transformed into one of Sofia's most desirable areas, known for its leafy streets, elegant residences, and trendy spots.

Why visit Lozenets? Imagine strolling down tree-lined boulevards, stopping at stylish cafes, and discovering unique boutiques. Lozenets is not just a place to see; it's a place to experience.

It offers a refined, yet relaxed atmosphere where you can enjoy Sofia's modern side while still being close to the city's ancient heart. Whether you're shopping, dining, or simply soaking up the ambiance, Lozenets offers a chic and enjoyable experience.

Location and getting there
Address: Lozenets, Sofia, Bulgaria.
GPS: 42.6662° N, 23.3184° E

How to get there: Lozenets is easily accessible from Sofia's city center. It's about a 10-minute drive or a quick metro ride to the Vitosha or European Union metro stops. Several bus and tram lines also serve the area.

The Best Time to Visit

The best time to visit Lozenets is during the spring and summer months (April to September), when the weather is pleasant and you can enjoy outdoor eating and strolling. Autumn also offers a beautiful scene with the changing leaves.

Hours of Opening and Admission Tickets Lozenets is a residential and commercial area, so there are no specific opening hours or admission tickets needed. Cafes, restaurants, and shops usually open from 9 a.m. to 10 p.m., but hours may vary.

What to do and see

South Park is a large and beautiful park, perfect for walking, jogging, or simply relaxing. The park features playgrounds, lakes, and plenty of green areas.

South Park's website

Tokuda Hospital Park: a smaller, serene park near Tokuda Hospital, great for a quiet stroll or a relaxing afternoon.

Bulgarevo Residence is a historical building that now houses offices and events, showing classic architecture amidst the modern vibe of Lozenets.

The Best Nearby Restaurants and Attractions

Sasa Asian Pub is a trendy spot offering a fusion of Asian food and cocktails.

Address: 18 Vitosha Boulevard
Website: Sasa Asian Pub

The Little Things is a cozy restaurant known for its charming setting and delicious European dishes.

Address: 37 Tsar Ivan Shishman Street
Website: The Little Things

Pod Lipite: serving traditional Bulgarian food in a rustic setting, perfect for experiencing local flavors.

Address: 1 Elin Pelin Street
Website: Pod Lipite

Nearby Attractions:

National Palace of Culture (NDK): A major cultural and conference center featuring various events, concerts, and exhibitions.

Address: 1 Bulgaria Blvd.

Website: NDK

Earth and Man National Museum: Focused on mining, this museum is excellent for those interested in natural history.

Address: 4 Cherni Vrah Blvd.
Website: Earth and Man National Museum

Photography Tips

Golden Hour: Capture stunning shots during the golden hour (shortly after sunrise and before sunset), when the light is soft and flattering.
Park Shots: For beautiful nature shots, utilize the greenery and calm of South Park and Tokuda Hospital Park.

Street Scenes: Lozenet's elegant streets and cafes make excellent backdrops for candid urban photos. building: Don't miss the unique blend of modern and historical buildings, which provides great contrast and interesting compositions.

Laws and rules

Public Behavior: Be respectful of local customs and rules. Public drunkenness and disruptive behavior are frowned upon.

Photography: Photography is usually allowed, but always ask permission before photographing people. Smoking: Smoking is banned in indoor public spaces, including restaurants and cafes. Designated smoking areas are provided.

Practical Information

Currency: The Bulgarian Lev (BGN) is the local currency. Credit cards are generally accepted, but it's good to have some cash for small purchases. Language: The official language is Bulgarian, but many people in the service industry know English. Safety: Lozenets is a safe neighborhood, but always be mindful of your belongings, especially in crowded places.

Interesting Facts

Vineyards Origin: The name Lozenets comes from the Bulgarian word for "vineyard," reflecting its history of vineyards and orchards.

Diplomatic Enclave: Lozenets is home to several embassies and diplomatic residences, adding to its upscale and foreign ambiance.

Modern Hub: The area has become a hotspot for young workers and creatives, making it one of the trendiest parts of Sofia.

Lozenets offers a perfect mix of upscale living and trendy cafes, making it a must-visit neighborhood in Sofia. From its beautiful parks and stylish restaurants to its chic boutiques and cultural attractions, Lozenets offers a unique and enjoyable experience for all visitors. Whether you're strolling through South Park, having a meal at a cozy cafe, or exploring the area's rich history, Lozenets is sure to leave a lasting impression.

Traveler Steves

Chapter five

Historic Sites and Cultural Attractions

Alexander Nevsky Cathedral

Alexander Nevsky Cathedral was built between 1882 and 1912 in honor of the Russian soldiers who died fighting for Bulgaria's freedom during the Russo-Turkish War (1877–1888). The cathedral, named after Saint Alexander Nevsky, a revered Russian prince, represents Bulgaria's gratitude to Russia.

The architectural design mixes Neo-Byzantine and Russian Revival styles, featuring stunning domes, intricate mosaics, and lavish interior decorations.

Why visit Alexander Nevsky Cathedral? Imagine stepping into a world where history, art, and faith converge. The cathedral's grand size and exquisite details leave a lasting impression. The church provides a profound experience, from its golden domes shining in the sunlight to its serene and awe-inspiring interior. Whether you're exploring the art and building or simply soaking in the atmosphere, Alexander Nevsky Cathedral is a place of beauty and reflection.

Location and getting there

Address: Alexander Nevsky Square, Sofia, Bulgaria. GPS: 42.6959° N, 23.3320° E

How to Get There: The cathedral is centrally situated and easily accessible. It's about a 10-minute walk from Serdika Metro Station. You can also take a cab or ride-sharing service, or use buses and trams that stop nearby.

The Best Time to Visit

The best time to visit Alexander Nevsky Cathedral is during the spring and summer months (April to September), when the weather is nice. However, the cathedral's beauty shines year-round, with smaller crowds in the winter. Early mornings or late afternoons are ideal for avoiding peak tourist times and catching beautiful light for photography.

Hours of Opening and Admission Tickets

Opening Hours: Every day from 7 a.m. to 7 p.m. Admission Tickets: Entry to the church is free. However, there is a small fee (around 10 BGN) for entering the crypt, which houses a remarkable collection of religious art and artifacts.

What to do and see

Explore the Cathedral: Marvel at the grand exterior with its golden domes and detailed architectural details. Step inside to experience the serene and majestic interior, adorned with beautiful mosaics, paintings, and icons. The main dome features a stunning image of Christ Pantocrator.

Visit the Crypt: Located beneath the cathedral, the crypt holds an amazing collection of Orthodox Christian art, including icons, frescoes, and religious artifacts. It's a must-see for art and history lovers. Attend a Service: If you're interested in experiencing the spiritual side of the cathedral, check the schedule for services and attend one to watch the rituals and chants of Eastern Orthodox worship.

The Best Nearby Restaurants and Attractions

Sasa Asian Pub is a trendy spot offering a fusion of Asian food and cocktails.

Address: 18 Vitosha Boulevard
Website: Sasa Asian Pub

Made in Home is known for its cozy setting and delicious Bulgarian and international dishes.

Address: 30A Angel Kanchev Street
Website: Made at Home

Moma Bulgarian Food & Wine is a beautiful restaurant that serves traditional Bulgarian cuisine.

Address: 28 Solunska Street
Website: Moma Bulgarian Food & Wine

Nearby Attractions:

National Gallery for Foreign Art: Explore a diverse collection of foreign art.

Address: 1 Alexander Nevsky Square
Website: National Gallery

Sofia University St. Kliment Ohridski is Bulgaria's oldest and most prestigious university, with beautiful architecture and a rich past.

Address: 15 Tsar Osvoboditel Boulevard
Sofia University's website

Sofia Past Museum: Discover Sofia's rich history and cultural heritage.

Address: 1 Banski Square
Website: Sofia History Museum

Photography Tips

Golden Hour: Capture stunning shots during the golden hour (shortly after sunrise and before sunset), when the light is soft and flattering. Interior Shots: Use a tripod and low ISO settings for clear and detailed shots of the interior. Be aware of the lighting and respect any photography restrictions. Details: Focus on the intricate details of the mosaics, frescoes, and architectural features for unique and compelling pictures.

Laws and rules

Please respect the site: Alexander Nevsky Cathedral is an ongoing place of worship. Dress modestly and be respectful of ongoing services and worshippers.

Photography: Photography is usually allowed, but avoid using flash inside the cathedral to preserve the artwork. Always follow the posted rules. Quiet and Respect: To preserve the peaceful atmosphere, maintain a respectful noise level inside the church.

Practical Information

Currency: The Bulgarian Lev (BGN) is the local currency. Credit cards are generally accepted, but it's good to have some cash for small purchases. Language: The official language is Bulgarian, but many people in the service industry know English. Safety: Alexander Nevsky Cathedral and its surroundings are usually safe, but always be mindful of your belongings, especially in crowded areas.

Interesting Facts

Architectural Masterpiece: The church is one of the largest Eastern Orthodox cathedrals in the world, with a capacity of 10,000 people.

Historical Significance: The cathedral was built to honor the Russian soldiers who died fighting for Bulgaria's freedom.

Cultural Treasure: The crypt houses one of Bulgaria's most extensive collections of Orthodox Christian art, making it a treasure trove for art lovers.

Alexander Nevsky Cathedral stands as a testament to Sofia's rich past, architectural grandeur, and spiritual depth. From its golden domes to its intricate mosaics, every detail of the church tells a story of faith, resilience, and artistry.

Whether you're exploring the majestic interior, visiting the crypt, or simply admiring the church from the outside, Alexander Nevsky Church offers an experience that is both awe-inspiring and deeply moving.

The National Palace of Culture

The National Palace of Culture, or NDK, was inaugurated in 1981 to honor Bulgaria's 1300th anniversary. It was the brainchild of Lyudmila Zhivkova, daughter of then-leader Todor Zhivkov, who envisioned a grand venue that would host cultural events and improve Bulgaria's cultural standing. The building, designed by architect Alexander Barov, is one of the largest multifunctional complexes in

Southeastern Europe, having striking brutalist architecture with a touch of elegance.

Why visit the National Palace of Culture? Imagine attending a world-class concert, exploring a modern art exhibition, or watching a thought-provoking theater performance, all under one roof. The NDK is a melting pot of artistic and cultural expression, holding events that cater to all tastes and interests. Whether you're an art lover, a music enthusiast, or just looking for a unique experience, the NDK offers a lively and enriching environment.

Location and getting there

Address: 1 Bulgaria Blvd., 1463 NDK, Sofia, Bulgaria
GPS: 42.6858° N, 23.3175° E

How to Get There: The National Palace of Culture is centrally placed and easily accessible. The nearest metro stop is NDK, which is right next to the complex. You can also reach the NDK by different bus and tram lines. If you're driving, there are parking facilities available nearby.

The Best Time to Visit

The best time to visit the National Palace of Culture depends on your interests. The NDK hosts events year-round, so check the schedule for concerts, exhibitions, and festivals that match your visit. Spring and fall are particularly vibrant times, with many cultural events and pleasant weather for exploring the surrounding areas.

Hours of Opening and Admission Tickets

Hours of Opening: The NDK is usually open from 9 a.m. to 6 p.m. for exhibitions and office hours. Event times vary according to the schedule. Admission Tickets: Ticket prices change based on the event. For individual shows, concerts, or exhibitions, check the NDK website or ticketing platforms for pricing and availability.

What to do and see

Attend a Concert or Performance: The NDK is renowned for its acoustics and hosts a range of musical performances, including classical concerts, rock shows, and jazz evenings. For more information, check the event schedule.

Explore Art Exhibitions: The complex regularly hosts contemporary art exhibitions, showcasing works by both local and foreign artists. The shows cover a range of mediums, from painting and sculpture to digital art. Visit the Theaters: The NDK houses several theaters that show diverse productions, from classic plays to modern performances. Enjoy a night of drama, comedy, or avant-garde theater.

Relax in the Park: The NDK is surrounded by a beautiful park with fountains, sculptures, and walking tracks. It's a wonderful spot for a leisurely stroll or a relaxing break.

The Best Nearby Restaurants and Attractions

Restaurants:
Sasa Asian Pub is a trendy spot offering a fusion of Asian food and cocktails.

Address: 18 Vitosha Boulevard
Website: Sasa Asian Pub

Made in Home is known for its cozy setting and delicious Bulgarian and international dishes.

Address: 30A Angel Kanchev Street
Website: Made at Home

Moma Bulgarian Food & Wine is a beautiful restaurant that serves traditional Bulgarian cuisine.

Address: 28 Solunska Street
Website: Moma Bulgarian Food & Wine

Nearby Attractions:

Vitosha Boulevard: Sofia's main shopping and dining street, ideal for an evening stroll.

Website: Vitosha Boulevard

Earth and Man National Museum: Focused on mining, this museum is excellent for those interested in natural history.

Address: 4 Cherni Vrah Blvd.
Website: Earth and Man National Museum

The Ivan Vazov National Theatre is Bulgaria's national theater, offering a range of shows in a stunning neoclassical building.

Address: 5 Dyakon Ignatii Street
The National Theatre's website

Photography Tips

Golden Hour: Capture stunning shots of the NDK during the golden hour (shortly after sunrise and before sunset), when the light is soft and flattering. Exterior Shots: The building's brutalist architecture offers dramatic angles and intriguing compositions. Focus on the geometric lines and differences. Interior Shots: Use a wide-angle lens to capture the grandeur of the concert halls and exhibition spaces. Be aware of event-specific restrictions on photography.

Laws and rules

Respect the venue: The NDK is a cultural and public place. Be respectful of the events and exhibitions, and follow any guidelines given by the staff. Photography: Photography is usually allowed, but restrictions may apply during specific events. Always check and follow the rules.

Smoking: Smoking is banned inside the NDK. Designated smoking places are available outside.

Practical Information

Currency: The Bulgarian Lev (BGN) is the local currency. Credit cards are generally accepted, but it's good to have some cash for small purchases. Language: The official language is Bulgarian, but many people in the service industry know English. Safety: The NDK and its environs are generally safe.

However, always be mindful of your belongings, especially in crowded places.

Interesting Facts

Architectural Marvel: The NDK is one of the biggest conference and cultural centers in Southeastern Europe, with a total area of 123,000 square meters. Award-Winning: In 2005, the NDK earned the International Association of Congress Centers (AIPC) Apex Award for the world's best congress center. Cultural Hub: The NDK hosts over 300 events a year, including the Sofia Film Fest, the New Year's Music Festival, and the Sofia International Book Fair.

The National Palace of Culture is a cornerstone of Sofia's cultural scene, offering a lively mix of events and activities that cater to all tastes. From concerts and exhibitions to theatrical events and beautiful parks, the NDK is a place where art, culture, and community come together.

Whether you're attending a world-class performance, exploring modern art, or simply enjoying the vibrant atmosphere, the NDK promises an enriching and memorable experience. Plan your visit, check the event schedule, and immerse yourself in the heart of Sofia's cultural life.

Sofia History Museum

The Sofia History Museum is housed in the former Central Mineral Baths building, a stunning architectural gem that dates back to the early 20th century. The baths, until they closed in the 1980s, were a popular part of Sofia's community life. In 2015, after major renovations, the building reopened as the Sofia History Museum. The museum's collection spans thousands of years, showcasing artifacts from prehistoric times to the modern age, reflecting the city's evolution.

Why visit the Sofia History Museum? Imagine walking through galleries filled with ancient artifacts, medieval relics, and exhibits that narrate Sofia's change from a Thracian settlement to a bustling modern capital. The museum gives a comprehensive and captivating look at the city's history.

Whether you're marveling at the intricate details of a centuries-old icon or learning about Sofia's freedom from Ottoman rule, there's something here for everyone to discover.

Location and getting there
Address: 1 Banski Square, Sofia, Bulgaria
GPS: 42.7002° N, 23.3220° E

How to Get There: The Sofia History Museum is centrally placed and easily accessible. It's about a 10-minute walk from Serdika Metro Station. You can also get there by different bus and tram lines, with stops nearby. If you're driving, parking spaces are available in the vicinity.

The Best Time to Visit

The Sofia History Museum is a wonderful destination year-round. However, visiting during the spring and fall months (April to June and September to November) can be particularly pleasant due to the milder weather. Weekday mornings or late afternoons are best for avoiding crowds.

Hours of Opening and Admission Tickets

Hours of Opening:
Tuesday to Sunday: 10 a.m.–6 p.m.
Closed on Mondays
Admission Tickets:
Adults: 6 BGN
Students and seniors: two BGNs
Family ticket (2 adults and up to 3 children): 10 BGN

What to do and see

Explore the Permanent Exhibitions: The museum's permanent exhibitions cover a wide range of historical eras. Highlights include prehistoric artifacts, medieval treasures, and exhibits on Sofia's development through the ages.

Visit the Temporary Exhibitions: The museum hosts temporary exhibitions that focus on specific themes or eras, often showcasing rare artifacts and providing deeper insights into particular aspects of Sofia's history.
Enjoy the architecture. The museum itself is a work of art. The former Central Mineral Baths building features beautiful murals, intricate tile work, and

impressive domes, making it a wonderful backdrop for your visit.

The Best Nearby Restaurants and Attractions

Made in Home is known for its cozy setting and delicious Bulgarian and international dishes.

Address: 30A Angel Kanchev Street
Website: Made at Home

Moma Bulgarian Food & Wine is a beautiful restaurant that serves traditional Bulgarian cuisine.

Address: 28 Solunska Street
Website: Moma Bulgarian Food & Wine

Sasa Asian Pub is a trendy spot offering a fusion of Asian food and cocktails.

Address: 18 Vitosha Boulevard
Website: Sasa Asian Pub

Nearby Attractions:

Alexander Nevsky Cathedral is a stunning architectural gem, just a short walk away.

Address: Alexander Nevsky Square
Alexander Nevsky Cathedral's website

Vitosha Boulevard: Sofia's main shopping and dining street, ideal for an evening stroll.

Website: Vitosha Boulevard

National Art Gallery: Explore Bulgaria's rich artistic history.

Address: 1 Knyaz Alexander I Square
National Art Gallery's website:

Photography Tips

Interior Shots: The museum's stunning architecture offers excellent photo opportunities. Capture the intricate details of the tile work and paintings. Exhibit Close-Ups: Focus on individual artifacts to show their unique features and craftsmanship. Use a close-up lens for detailed shots. Natural Light: For well-lit and vibrant pictures, take advantage of the natural light streaming through the museum's windows.

Laws and rules

Respect the artifacts: Do not touch the exhibits. Many artifacts are fragile and need to be protected for future generations.
Photography: Photography is usually allowed, but flash photography may be prohibited. Always check for signs and follow the rules.

Quiet and Respect: To preserve the museum's serene mood and ensure a pleasant experience for all guests, maintain a respectful noise level.

Practical Information

Currency: The Bulgarian Lev (BGN) is the local currency. Credit cards are generally accepted, but it's good to have some cash for small purchases.
Language: The legal language is Bulgarian, but many of the museum's displays have English translations, and the staff often speaks English.

Safety: The Sofia History Museum is a safe and secure setting. However, always be mindful of your belongings, especially in crowded places.

Interesting Facts

Mineral Baths Heritage: The building that houses the museum was originally the Central Mineral Baths, a famous spot for Sofia's residents to relax and socialize.

Architectural Beauty: The museum's building is a fine example of early 20th-century architecture, combining aspects of Neo-Byzantine and Secessionist styles.
Diverse Collection: The museum's collection spans from prehistoric artifacts to modern items, giving a comprehensive look at Sofia's evolution.

The Sofia History Museum is a treasure trove of knowledge and beauty, offering a fascinating journey through the city's rich past. From its captivating exhibitions to its stunning architecture, the museum provides an engaging and educational experience for guests of all ages. Whether you're delving into old history, exploring medieval artifacts, or simply admiring the building itself, the Sofia History Museum promises a memorable visit.

Ancient Serdica Archaeological Complex

The Ancient Serdica Archaeological Complex is a treasure trove of history, showing the remains of the ancient city of Serdica. Founded by the Thracians and later expanded by the Romans, Serdica was a bustling urban center by the 1st century AD.

It became an important Roman city, favored by emperors like Constantine the Great, who once declared, "Serdica is my Rome." The complex includes remnants of streets, houses, baths, and an amphitheater, giving a glimpse into daily life in ancient times.

Why should you visit the Ancient Serdica Archaeological Complex? Picture yourself standing amidst ancient ruins, feeling the weight of history as you discover well-preserved Roman streets and buildings. This site offers a unique chance to see how the ancient city was laid out, with detailed information panels that bring the history to life. It's not just a place to see; it's a place to feel Sofia's ancient roots.

Location and getting there

Address: 1 Banski Square, Sofia, Bulgaria
GPS: 42.6986° N, 23.3223° E

How to Get There: The Ancient Serdica Archaeological Complex is centrally situated and easily accessible by public transportation. Serdika, which is right next to the site, is the closest metro stop. Buses and trams also stop close. If you're driving, parking is available in the area.

The Best Time to Visit

The complex is a wonderful destination year-round. However, spring and fall (April to June and September to November) are particularly pleasant times to visit due to the mild weather. Early mornings or late afternoons are best for avoiding the midday heat and crowds.

Hours of Opening and Admission Tickets
Hours of Opening:
Daily: 10 a.m.–6 p.m.
Admission Tickets:
Adults: 6 BGN
Students and seniors: two BGNs
Family ticket (2 adults and up to 3 children): 10 BGN

What to do and see

Explore the Ruins: Walk through Roman streets, houses, and public baths. Detailed information panels provide historical background and perspectives on ancient life.

Visit the Amphitheater: Discover the remnants of the Roman amphitheater, which once held gladiatorial games and public spectacles.

Interactive Displays: Enjoy interactive displays and exhibits that bring Serdica's past to life, including 3D reconstructions and multimedia presentations. Guided Tours: Join a guided tour to gain deeper insights from experienced guides who can share fascinating stories and facts about the site. The Best Nearby Restaurants and Attractions

Nearby Restaurants:

The Sense Hotel Rooftop Bar provides stunning views of Sofia, as well as a wide range of drinks and light meals.

Address: 16 Tsar Osvoboditel Blvd.
Website: Sense Hotel Rooftop Bar

Cosmos is a stylish restaurant known for its modern Bulgarian cuisine and creative dishes.

Address: 19 Lavele Street
Website: Cosmos

Hadjidraganovite Kashti: Offers traditional Bulgarian food in a lovely, historic setting.

Address: 75 Kozloduy Street
Website: Hadjidraganovite Kashti

Nearby Attractions:

St. George Rotunda: One of Sofia's oldest buildings, dating back to the 4th century and still used as a church.

Address: 2 Tsar Osvoboditel Blvd.
St. George Rotunda's website

Sofia History Museum: Provides a thorough look at Sofia's past, housed in the beautiful former Central Mineral Baths building.

Address: 1 Banski Square
Website: Sofia History Museum

The National Art Gallery, located nearby, showcases a rich collection of Bulgarian art.

Address: 1 Knyaz Alexander I Square
National Art Gallery's website:

Photography Tips

Golden Hour: Visit during the golden hour (shortly after sunrise or before sunset) to catch the ruins in beautiful, soft light.

Detail Shots: Focus on the intricate features of the ancient buildings and artifacts. Use a close-up lens for close-ups.

Wide Shots: Use a wide-angle lens to capture the expansive views of the archaeological site, giving a sense of scale and context.

Laws and rules

Respect the Ruins: Do not touch or climb on the ancient buildings. Many artifacts are fragile and need to be protected.

Photography: Photography is usually allowed, but avoid using flash, which can damage artifacts.

Quiet and Respect: To preserve the serene atmosphere and ensure a pleasant experience for all guests, maintain a respectful noise level.

Practical Information

Currency: The Bulgarian Lev (BGN) is the local currency. Credit cards are generally accepted, but it's good to have some cash for small purchases. Language: The official language is Bulgarian, but many of the information screens are in English, and the staff often speaks English.

The Ancient Serdica Archaeological Complex is a safe environment. However, always be mindful of your belongings, especially in crowded places.

Interesting Facts

Roman Heritage: Serdica was one of the most important cities in the Roman Empire, known for its strategic location and vibrant culture. Emperor Constantine: The Roman Emperor Constantine the Great had a palace in Serdica, which he frequently referred to as his favorite city.

Hidden Beneath: Much of the ancient city lies beneath modern Sofia, and excavations continue to reveal new discoveries.

The Ancient Serdica Archaeological Complex offers a fascinating journey through Sofia's rich and ancient past. From its well-preserved Roman streets and buildings to its interactive displays and informative panels, the site provides a comprehensive and engaging look at the city's history. Whether you're a history enthusiast, a curious traveler, or simply looking to explore something new, the Ancient Serdica Archaeological Complex promises an unforgettable experience.

Sofia Zoo

Sofia Zoo, established in 1888, is the oldest and largest zoo in Bulgaria. It began with a small animal collection but has grown significantly over the years, now housing over 2,000 animals from around 250 species. Located in the southern part of Sofia, the zoo covers 36 hectares, providing ample space for its diverse inhabitants and visitors alike.

Why visit the Sofia Zoo? Imagine spending the day wandering through lush, green spaces, meeting animals from all over the world. From majestic lions and playful monkeys to exotic birds and fascinating reptiles, Sofia Zoo offers a unique chance to observe and learn about wildlife in a well-maintained and educational setting.

It's a place where you can reconnect with nature and share memorable times with family and friends.

Location and getting there

Address: 1 Srebarna Street, Sofia, Bulgaria. GPS: 42.6544° N, 23.3161° E

How to Get There: Sofia Zoo is easily accessible by public transportation. You can take buses 88, 120, or

98, which stop near the zoo. If you're driving, there is ample parking available at the spot.

The Best Time to Visit

The best time to visit Sofia Zoo is during the spring and summer months (April to September), when the weather is warm and the animals are most busy. Early mornings or late afternoons are ideal for avoiding the heat of the day and having a leisurely visit.

Hours of Opening and Admission Tickets

Hours of Opening:
April to October: 9 a.m.–6 p.m.
November to March: 9 a.m.–5 p.m.
Admission Tickets:
Adults: 4 BGN
Children (up to 18 years): 2 BGN
Students and seniors: two BGNs
Family ticket (2 adults and up to 3 children): 10 BGN

What to do and see

Explore the Animal Exhibits: Sofia Zoo is home to a wide range of animals, including big cats like lions and tigers, primates, elephants, birds, reptiles, and many more. Each exhibit is intended to replicate the animals' natural habitats as closely as possible.

Educational Programs: For children and adults, the zoo offers educational programs and events. These programs are meant to raise awareness about wildlife conservation and provide fascinating insights into the animal kingdom.

Children's Playground: For younger guests, there is a well-equipped playground where kids can burn off some energy while parents take a break. Picnic places: Bring your own food and enjoy a picnic in one of the designated places within the zoo. It's a wonderful way to relax and make the most of your time.

The Best Nearby Restaurants and Attractions

Sasa Asian Pub is a trendy spot offering a fusion of Asian food and cocktails.

Address: 18 Vitosha Boulevard
Website: Sasa Asian Pub

Made in Home is known for its cozy setting and delicious Bulgarian and international dishes.

Address: 30A Angel Kanchev Street
Website: Made at Home

Moma Bulgarian Food & Wine is a beautiful restaurant that serves traditional Bulgarian cuisine.

Address: 28 Solunska Street
Website: Moma Bulgarian Food & Wine

Nearby Attractions:

Vitosha Boulevard: Sofia's main shopping and dining street, ideal for an evening stroll.

Website: Vitosha Boulevard

The National Museum of the Past, located nearby, offers extensive exhibits on Bulgaria's past from ancient times to the present.

Address: 16 Vitoshko Lale Street. The National Museum of History's website

Photography Tips

Natural Light: Visit during the early morning or late afternoon when the natural light is softer, perfect for photographing animals.

Close-ups: Use a zoom lens to catch detailed shots of the animals without disturbing them. For compelling shots, focus on their eyes and expressions.

Patience: Animals may not always pose for the right shot. Be patient and ready to catch moments as they happen naturally.

Laws and rules

Respect the animals. Do not feed or bother the animals. Follow all written signs and guidelines. Stay on Paths: Remain on marked paths to ensure your and the animals' safety.

No Flash Photography: Avoid using flash photography, as it can scare the animals.

Practical Information

Currency: The Bulgarian Lev (BGN) is the local currency. Credit cards are accepted at the zoo, but it's good to have some cash for small purchases. Language: The official language is Bulgarian, but many staff members know English.

Safety: Sofia Zoo is a safe and family-friendly setting. Always keep an eye on your belongings and watch children at all times.

Interesting Facts

Sofia Zoo is Bulgaria's oldest zoo, with a rich history spanning over 130 years.

Diverse Collection: The zoo houses over 2,000 animals from around 250 species, making it one of the most diverse collections in the area.

Conservation Efforts: Sofia Zoo actively participates in various conservation programs and works to teach the public about wildlife preservation.

Sofia Zoo offers a delightful and educational experience for guests of all ages. From its diverse animal exhibits to its engaging teaching programs, the zoo provides a perfect blend of fun and learning. Whether you're exploring the lush grounds, watching exotic animals, or enjoying a picnic with family, Sofia Zoo promises a memorable day out.

Chapter six

Hidden Gems

The Bells Monument

The Bells Monument, also known as "Kambanite," was opened in 1979 by Lyudmila Zhivkova, the daughter of the then Bulgarian leader Todor Zhivkov. It was made to commemorate the International Year of the Child, declared by UNESCO. The monument consists of numerous bells given by countries from around the world, each representing the hopes and dreams of that nation's children. The site has since become a symbol of peace and world unity.

Why visit the Bells Monument? Imagine standing in a tranquil park, surrounded by the gentle chime of bells from every corner of the world. The Bells Monument isn't just a site to see; it's a place to reflect on the universal ideals of peace, friendship, and the importance of nurturing the younger generations. It's a unique and serene destination that offers both a historical viewpoint and a hopeful outlook for the future.

Location and getting there

Address: Bulevard Samokovsko Shose, 1137 Sofia, Bulgaria

GPS: 42.6225° N, 23.3777° E

How to Get There: The Bells Monument is located about 15 kilometers southeast of Sofia's city center. You can get there by taking bus 111 or a taxi. If you're driving, there is ample parking available at the spot.

The Best Time to Visit

The best time to visit The Bells Monument is during the spring and summer months (April to September), when the weather is warm and the nearby park is lush and green. Early mornings or late afternoons are best for enjoying the tranquility of the site.

Hours of Opening and Admission Tickets
Opening Hours: The Bells Monument is open to the public 24/7.

Admission Tickets: There is no admission fee to visit the Bells Monument. It's free for all guests.

What to do and see

Explore the Monument: Walk around the monument and admire the diverse collection of bells from different countries. Each bell has a unique design and inscription, representing its country of origin.

Ring the Bells: Many of the bells can be rung by guests. Take a moment to listen to the unique sounds of each bell, creating a peaceful and harmonious symphony. Reflect in the Park: The monument is set within a beautiful park, perfect for a leisurely stroll, a picnic, or simply sitting and thinking about the monument's message of peace and unity.

The Best Nearby Restaurants and Attractions

Vitosha Park Hotel Restaurant offers a range of Bulgarian and international dishes in a comfortable setting.

Address: 1 Rosario Street, Sofia
Vitosha Park Hotel's website:

Restaurant Pri Yafata is known for its traditional Bulgarian cuisine and cozy setting.

Address: 69 Vasil Levski Blvd., Sofia
Website: Pri Yafata

Made in Home is a stylish restaurant offering a mix of Bulgarian and foreign dishes.

The address is 30A Angel Kanchev Street, Sofia.
Website: Made at Home

Nearby Attractions:

Sofia Ring Mall is a large shopping center with a range of stores, dining options, and entertainment facilities.

Address: 214 Okolovrasten Pat, Sofia
Website: Sofia Ring Mall

Vitosha Mountain is a popular location for hiking, skiing, and enjoying nature, located just a short drive from the monument.

Website: Vitosha Mountain

Photography Tips

Golden Hour: Visit during the golden hour (shortly after sunrise and before dusk) for soft, warm light that enhances the beauty of the monument and park. Close-ups: Focus on the intricate features and inscriptions on the bells. Use a close-up lens for detailed shots.

Wide Shots: Capture the entire landmark in its serene setting. A wide-angle lens will help you include the nearby park in your shots.

Reflections: For a creative perspective, use any water features or wet surfaces to catch the bells' reflections.

Laws and rules

Respect the memorial. Do not deface the bells or other parts. Treat the site with the respect it deserves. Quiet and Respect: To preserve a peaceful environment, maintain a respectful noise level. Leave No Trace: To keep the park clean, make sure you bring all of your belongings and any trash with you.

Practical Information

Currency: The Bulgarian Lev (BGN) is the local currency. It's always beneficial to have some cash for small purchases.

Language: The official language is Bulgarian, but many people know English, especially in tourist areas.

Safety: The Bells Monument is a safe and family-friendly spot. Always keep an eye on your belongings and watch your children.

Interesting Facts

The Bells Monument was part of UNESCO's initiative to promote peace and unity through cultural and educational projects.

Global Representation: The monument features bells from over 100 countries, each individually designed and inscribed.

Symbol of Hope: The site is often used for events and ceremonies that support peace and international cooperation.

The Bells Monument is more than just a monument; it's a powerful symbol of peace, togetherness, and hope for the future. From its beautiful bells and serene park setting to its profound message, it offers a unique and reflective experience for all guests. The Bells

Monument promises a memorable visit, whether you're exploring the bells, having a peaceful moment in the park, or simply taking in the monument's beauty.

Vrana Palace

Vrana Palace was built in the early 20th century as a royal palace for Tsar Ferdinand I of Bulgaria. The construction began in 1904 and was finished in several stages, with the palace acting as a primary residence for the Bulgarian royal family until the monarchy was abolished in 1946.

The estate, which includes extensive gardens and parklands, was intended to be a private retreat, blending luxury with nature. Today, it is owned by the royal family and serves as a museum and cultural site.

Why visit Vrana Palace? Imagine strolling through beautifully landscaped grounds, discovering elegantly decorated rooms, and stepping back in time to an era of royal grandeur.

Vrana Palace isn't just a historical site; it's a live museum that offers insight into Bulgaria's royal heritage. From the architectural beauty of the palace to the tranquility of its gardens, there's something here to captivate every guest.

Location and getting there

Address: Bulevard Tsarigradsko Shose 381, 1582 Sofia, Bulgaria

GPS: 42.6332° N, 23.4240° E

How to Get There: Vrana Palace is located about 11 kilometers southeast of Sofia's city center. You can reach it by car or cab, and there are also buses (lines 5 and 505) that stop near the estate. If you're driving, there is ample parking available on-site.

The Best Time to Visit

The best time to visit Vrana Palace is during the spring

and summer months (April to September), when the grounds are in full bloom and the weather is pleasant. Early mornings or late afternoons are best for avoiding the midday heat and enjoying the serene environment.

Hours of Opening and Admission Tickets

Hours of Opening:
Saturday and Sunday: 10 a.m.–4 p.m.
Closed on weekends.
Admission Tickets:
Adults: 5 BGN
Students and seniors: two BGNs
Children under 7 are free.

What to do and see

Explore the Palace: Take a guided tour of the palace to learn about its history and building. Marvel at the beautifully decorated rooms, the intricate woodwork, and the elegant furniture that reflect the royal family's lifestyle.

Stroll Through the Gardens: The gardens at Vrana Palace are a highlight, containing a wide variety of plant species, manicured lawns, and serene ponds. The parkland covers over 960 acres and includes walking paths, making it ideal for a leisurely stroll or a picnic.

Visit the Museum: The palace houses a small museum with exhibits on the Bulgarian royal family's history, including personal artifacts, photos, and documents. Attend Cultural Events: Vrana Palace rarely hosts cultural events, including concerts, exhibitions, and theatrical performances. Check the schedule to see if any events coincide with your stay.

The Best Nearby Restaurants and Attractions

Pod Lipite is known for its traditional Bulgarian cuisine and cozy setting.

Address: 1 Elin Pelin Street, Sofia.
Website: Pod Lipite

Made in Home offers a mix of Bulgarian and foreign dishes in a stylish setting.

The address is 30A Angel Kanchev Street, Sofia.
Website: Made at Home

Sasa Asian Pub is a trendy spot with a fusion of Asian food and cocktails.

Address: 18 Vitosha Boulevard, Sofia.
Website: Sasa Asian Pub

Nearby Attractions:

Sofia Ring Mall is a large shopping center with a range of stores, dining options, and entertainment facilities.

Address: 214 Okolovrasten Pat, Sofia
Website: Sofia Ring Mall

Vitosha Mountain, a famous destination for hiking, skiing, and enjoying nature, is located a short drive from the palace.

Website: Vitosha Mountain

Photography Tips

Golden Hour: To capture stunning shots of the palace and gardens during the golden hour (shortly after sunrise and before sunset), use soft, warm light. Close-ups: Focus on the intricate details of the palace's design and the vibrant flowers in the gardens. Wide Shots: To capture the expansive gardens and the grandeur of the palace, use a wide-angle lens. Reflections: Take advantage of the ponds and water features to catch beautiful reflections.

Laws and rules

Respect the site. Do not touch or damage any objects or plants. Follow all written signs and guidelines. Photography: Photography is usually allowed, but avoid using flash inside the palace to protect the artifacts.

Quiet and Respect: To preserve the tranquility of the palace and grounds, maintain a respectful noise level.

Practical Information

Currency: The Bulgarian Lev (BGN) is the local currency. Credit cards are allowed at the ticket office, but it's good to have some cash for small purchases. Language: Although Bulgarian is the official language, many staff members speak English and can provide information and assistance.

Safety: Vrana Palace is a safe and family-friendly environment. Always keep an eye on your belongings and watch your children.

Interesting Facts

Royal Residence: Vrana Palace was the main residence of the Bulgarian royal family from its completion until the monarchy was abolished in 1946. Botanical Diversity: The gardens at Vrana Palace feature over 400 plant types, including many rare and exotic plants.

Cultural Events: The palace grounds are used for different cultural events, including concerts, exhibitions, and performances, contributing to Sofia's vibrant cultural scene.

Vrana Palace offers a unique mix of historical grandeur, architectural beauty, and natural tranquility.

From its elegantly decorated rooms and intriguing museum exhibits to its expansive gardens and cultural events, the palace provides an enriching and enjoyable experience for all guests. Whether you're exploring the past of Bulgaria's royal family, strolling through the lush gardens, or attending a cultural event, Vrana Palace promises a memorable visit.

Borisova Gradina Park

Borisova Gradina, or Boris' Garden, was created in 1884 and named after Tsar Boris III of Bulgaria. The park was designed by several famous gardeners and landscapers over the years, each adding their own unique touch. The park features beautifully landscaped gardens, walking paths, sports facilities, and historic monuments, making it a favorite spot for both relaxation and leisure.

Why visit Borisova Gradina? Imagine strolling along tree-lined avenues, relaxing by tranquil ponds, or having a picnic on lush green lawns. Borisova Gradina isn't just a park; it's a lively urban oasis where you can escape the hustle and bustle of the city.

Whether you're an avid jogger, a nature lover, or someone wanting a peaceful spot to read a book, this park has something for everyone.

Location and getting there

Adresse: Knyaz Borisova Gradina, Sofia, Bulgaria
GPS: 42.6864° N, 23.3431° E

How to Get There: Borisova Gradina is centrally located and easily accessible by public transportation. The closest metro stations are "Vasil Levski Stadium" and "Joliot-Curie." Buses and trams also stop near the park's gates. If you're driving, there are parking facilities available nearby.

The Best Time to Visit

The best time to visit Borisova Gradina is during the spring and summer months (April to September), when the gardens are in full bloom and the weather is nice. Early mornings and late afternoons offer cooler temperatures and a more peaceful environment. Autumn also gives a beautiful setting with colorful foliage.

Hours of Opening and Admission Tickets

Opening Hours: Borisova Gradina is open 24/7. Admission Tickets: Entry to the park is free of charge.

What to do and see

Explore the Gardens: Wander through the meticulously landscaped gardens, which contain a wide variety of plants and flowers. The rose garden and the Japanese garden are particularly beautiful. Visit the landmarks: Discover historic landmarks such as the Soviet Army Monument, the Eagles' Bridge, and the Vasil Levski Monument, each telling a story from Bulgaria's past.

Enjoy Recreational Activities: Take advantage of the park's sports facilities, including tennis areas, football fields, and running tracks. There's also a children's playground for the little ones.

Relax by the Ponds: Find a peaceful spot by one of the park's ponds, where you can feed the ducks, enjoy a lunch, or simply rest and take in the scenery.

The Best Nearby Restaurants and Attractions

Park Bar: A relaxing spot offering drinks and light meals with a view of the park.

Address: 14 Shipka Street, Sofia
Website: Park Bar

Pod Lipite is known for its traditional Bulgarian cuisine and cozy setting.

Address: 1 Elin Pelin Street, Sofia.
Website: Pod Lipite

Made in Home offers a mix of Bulgarian and foreign dishes in a stylish setting.

The address is 30A Angel Kanchev Street, Sofia. Website: Made at Home

Nearby Attractions:

Sofia University is one of the oldest and most famous universities in Bulgaria, located near the park.

Address: 15 Tsar Osvoboditel Blvd., Sofia Sofia University's website

Vasil Levski National Stadium is Bulgaria's largest stadium, hosting a variety of sporting events and concerts.

Address: 38 Evlogi and Hristo Georgiev Blvd., Sofia Website: National Stadium

Photography Tips

Golden Hour: Visit the gardens and monuments during the golden hour (shortly after sunrise and before dusk) for soft, warm light that enhances their beauty.

Close-ups: Focus on the intricate details of flowers, plants, and historical landmarks. Use a close-up lens for detailed shots.

Wide Shots: Capture the vast lawns, tree-lined roads, and scenic ponds. A wide-angle lens will help you include more of the park's beauty in your shot. Reflection Shots: Use the park's ponds to catch beautiful reflections of the surrounding greenery and monuments.

Laws and rules

Respect the Park: Do not litter or damage the plants and structures. Follow all written signs and guidelines. Respect and Quiet: To protect the park's peaceful atmosphere, maintain a respectful noise level. Pets: Dogs are welcome but must be kept on a lead. Always clean up after your pets.

Practical Information

Currency: The Bulgarian Lev (BGN) is the local currency. It's always beneficial to have some cash for small purchases at nearby cafes or sellers. Language: The official language is Bulgarian, but many people in Sofia know English.

Safety: Borisova Gradina is a safe and family-friendly environment. However, always keep an eye on your belongings, especially in crowded places.

Interesting Facts

Borisova Gradina, the oldest and largest park in Sofia, has a history dating back to 1884.

Historical Monuments: The park is home to several important historical monuments, each reflecting significant events in Bulgarian history. Diverse Flora: The park offers a wide variety of plant species, including rare and exotic flowers in the Rose Garden and Japanese Garden.

Borisova Gradina Park offers a perfect blend of natural beauty, historical significance, and recreational possibilities. From its carefully landscaped gardens and tranquil ponds to its historic monuments and sports facilities, the park provides a serene and enjoyable escape from the city's hustle and bustle. Whether you're exploring the gardens, having a picnic, or participating in recreational activities, Borisova Gradina promises a delightful experience.

Mineral Baths and Spas

Sofia's rich history with mineral baths goes back to the Thracian and Roman periods, when the healing properties of the city's natural springs were first discovered and utilized. The mineral baths became a cornerstone of social and therapeutic life during the Roman era, and their fame continued through the centuries.

The iconic Central Mineral Baths building, built in the early 20th century, stands as a testament to this enduring tradition. Sofia continues to embrace its ancient history today, with modern spa facilities that blend historical charm with contemporary luxury.

Why visit Sofia's mineral pools and spas? Imagine

slipping into warm, mineral-rich waters, feeling the stress melt away as you rest and rejuvenate. These baths offer more than just relaxation; they provide therapeutic benefits that can ease a range of ailments, from joint pain to skin conditions. Whether you're looking for a tranquil vacation, a wellness treatment, or a cultural experience, Sofia's mineral baths and spas have something for everyone.

Top Mineral Baths and Spas in Sofia

Central Mineral Baths (now Sofia History Museum)

Location: 1 Banski Square, Sofia, Bulgaria
GPS: 42.7002° N, 23.3220° E

Overview: The Central Mineral Baths building, now home to the Sofia History Museum, is a beautiful example of early 20th-century design. While the baths themselves are no longer operational, the museum offers a fascinating glimpse into Sofia's past, including its thermal bathing customs.

Website: Sofia History Museum

Bankya Mineral Baths

Locations: Bankya, Sofia, Bulgaria
GPS: 42.7061° N, 23.1778° E

Overview: Located in the picturesque town of Bankya, just outside Sofia, these baths are famous for their healing properties. The mineral water here is particularly helpful for cardiovascular and respiratory conditions. Bankya also boasts beautiful parks and walking trails, making it a wonderful day trip destination.

Best Time to Visit: In Bankya, the spring and summer months are ideal for combining your spa visit with outdoor activities.

Admission tickets: Prices vary depending on the treatment. The basic registration fee is approximately 10 BGN.

How to Get There: From Sofia, Bankya can be reached by train or bus. It's a 30-minute trip from the city center.

Website: Bankya Mineral Baths
Velingrad
Location: Velingrad, Bulgaria (nearly 130 km from Sofia)
GPS: 42.0285° N, 23.9914° E

Overview: Known as the "Spa Capital of the Balkans,"

Velingrad offers some of the best spa facilities in Bulgaria. The town has numerous hotels and wellness centers, each with a variety of mineral baths and therapeutic treatments.

Best Time to Visit: Velingrad is a year-round destination, but spring and fall offer pleasant weather for outdoor exploration.

Admission tickets: Prices vary widely depending on the spa. Day passes are typically issued at 20 BGN. How to Get There: Velingrad is reachable by bus or train from Sofia. The trip takes approximately 2–3 hours.

Velingrad Spa's website

What to do and see

Relax in Mineral Baths: Enjoy the soothing waters of Sofia's mineral baths, known for their therapeutic qualities. Spend a few hours soaking and resting. Experience Spa Treatments: Treat yourself to a variety of spa services, including massages, mud treatments, and aromatherapy, designed to enhance your relaxation and health.

Explore Surrounding Areas: Combine your spa visit with a tour of the nearby sites. In Bankya, discover the town's parks and trails. In Velingrad, enjoy the natural beauty of the Rhodope Mountains.

The Best Nearby Restaurants and Attractions

Pri Yafata offers classic Bulgarian cuisine in a cozy setting.

Address: 69 Vasil Levski Blvd., Sofia
Website: Pri Yafata

Made in Home is known for its innovative dishes and stylish surroundings.

The address is 30A Angel Kanchev Street, Sofia.
Website: Made at Home

Pod Lipite offers authentic Bulgarian dishes in a historic setting.

Address: 1 Elin Pelin Street, Sofia.
Website: Pod Lipite

Nearby Attractions:

Sofia Past Museum: Learn about the city's rich history and bathing traditions.

Address: 1 Banski Square, Sofia
Website: Sofia History Museum

Vitosha Boulevard: Explore Sofia's main shopping and eating street.

Website: Vitosha Boulevard

Photography Tips

Golden Hour: To capture the beauty of the spa facilities and nearby nature during the golden hour, use soft, warm light.

features: Focus on the architectural features of historic bath buildings and the serene ambiance of modern spas.

Wide Shots: To capture expansive spa environments and lush nearby landscapes, use a wide-angle lens. Reflection Shots: Use the water features to make beautiful reflection photos.

Laws and rules

Respect the Facilities: Follow all written rules and guidelines to ensure a safe and enjoyable experience for everyone.

Photography: Always ask permission before taking photos inside spa facilities, as privacy is important. Quiet and Respect: To preserve the tranquil environment, maintain a quiet and respectful demeanor to protect the tranquil environment.

Practical Information

Currency: The Bulgarian Lev (BGN) is the local currency. Credit cards are generally accepted, but it's good to have some cash for small purchases. Language: The official language is Bulgarian, but many spa staff know English.

Safety: Sofia's spas are safe and well-maintained. Always follow the safety instructions and guidelines given by the staff.

Interesting Facts

Ancient Tradition: Sofia's mineral baths have been used for their healing qualities since Thracian and Roman times.

Diverse Waters: The mineral composition of the

waters varies by location, each with its own unique therapeutic benefits.

Cultural Heritage: The Central Mineral Baths building is an important cultural and architectural landmark in Sofia.

Sofia's mineral baths and spas offer a unique blend of relaxation, wellness, and cultural history. From the historic charm of the Central Mineral Baths to the modern luxury of Velingrad's spa resorts, there's something for everyone wanting rejuvenation and tranquility. Whether you're soaking in mineral-rich waters, indulging in a spa treatment, or exploring the beautiful surroundings, Sofia's health havens promise an unforgettable experience.

Boyana Church

Boyana Church, located on the outskirts of Sofia, is a medieval Bulgarian Orthodox church that dates back to the late 10th and early 11th centuries. The church is famous for its exquisite frescoes, which were added in 1259 and are considered some of the most important examples of medieval Eastern European art.

These frescoes predate the Italian Renaissance by a century and are notable for their realism and detailed human expressions, giving valuable insights into the era's artistic and cultural practices.

Why visit Boyana Church? Imagine stepping into a small, ancient church and being surrounded by vivid, centuries-old frescoes that tell stories of saints, angels, and historical people. The Boyana Church isn't just a building; it's a time capsule that protects the artistry and spiritual devotion of medieval Bulgaria. From its architectural beauty to its breathtaking frescoes, this church offers a unique and enriching experience that will leave you with a deeper understanding of Bulgaria's heritage.

Location and getting there

Address: 1-3 Boyansko Ezero Str., Sofia, Bulgaria
GPS: 42.6441° N, 23.2696° E

How to Get There: Boyana Church is situated in the Boyana district, about 8 kilometers from Sofia's city center. You can reach it by car or cab, and there are also buses (lines 64 and 107) that stop near the church. If you're driving, there is limited parking available nearby.

The Best Time to Visit

The best time to visit Boyana Church is during the spring and summer months (April to September), when the weather is pleasant and the surrounding grounds are in bloom. Early mornings or late afternoons offer cooler temperatures and fewer crowds, making for a more peaceful stay.

Hours of Opening and Admission Tickets

Hours of Opening:
Tuesday to Sunday: 9 AM - 5:30 PM
Closed on Mondays
Admission Tickets:
Adults: 10 BGN
Students and seniors: two BGNs
Children under 7 are free.

What to do and see

Explore the Frescoes: Boyana Church's main attraction is its stunning frescoes. Spend time admiring the detailed and expressive paintings that portray biblical scenes, saints, and historical people. Each fresco is a masterpiece, rich with meaning and history. Learn the History: Join a guided tour to gain greater insights into the church's history, architecture, and the significance of its frescoes. Knowledgeable guides can provide an intriguing background and answer any questions you may have.

Enjoy the Gardens: The church is surrounded by a peaceful garden, great for a leisurely stroll or quiet reflection. The well-maintained greenery enhances the serene atmosphere of the place.

The Best Nearby Restaurants and Attractions

Villa Spaggo offers delicious Italian food in a cozy and elegant setting.

Address: 19 Boyansko Ezero Str., Sofia
Website: Villa Spaggo

Restaurant Boyana is known for its traditional Bulgarian dishes and warm welcome.

Address: 3 Belovodski Pat Str., Sofia
Website: Restaurant Boyana

Made in Home is a stylish restaurant offering a mix of Bulgarian and foreign dishes.

The address is 30A Angel Kanchev Street, Sofia.
Website: Made at Home

Nearby Attractions:

The National Museum of the Past, located nearby, offers extensive exhibits on Bulgaria's past, from ancient times to the present.

Address: 16 Vitoshko Lale St., Sofia.
The National Museum of History's website

Vitosha Mountain is perfect for climbing and enjoying panoramic views of Sofia. The mountain's proximity makes it an ideal spot for nature lovers.

Website: Vitosha Mountain

Photography Tips

Natural Light: Use the natural light streaming through the small windows to catch the vivid colors and details of the frescoes.

Close-ups: Focus on the intricate details of the paintings. A macro lens can help catch the fine lines and expressions.

Wide Shots: To show the context of the frescoes within the architectural space, capture the full interior. Exterior Shots: Don't forget to picture the charming church exterior and its serene garden setting.

Laws and rules

Respect the artwork. Do not touch the paintings. Their preservation is important, and oils from hands can cause damage.

Photography: Flash photography is forbidden inside the church to protect the frescoes. Always check for written guidelines.

Respect and Quiet: To preserve the peaceful atmosphere of this sacred place, maintain a respectful noise level.

Practical Information

Currency: The Bulgarian Lev (BGN) is the local currency. Credit cards are allowed at the ticket office, but it's good to have some cash for small purchases. Language: The official language is Bulgarian, but many guides and staff members know English.

Safety: Boyana Church is a safe and family-friendly setting. However, always keep an eye on your things.

Interesting Facts

UNESCO Heritage: Boyana Church was inscribed as a UNESCO World Heritage Site in 1979, recognizing its great cultural value.

Artistic Innovation: The paintings in Boyana Church are noted for their realism and emotional depth, predating the Italian Renaissance by a century. Royal Connection: The church was commissioned by the Bulgarian lord Kaloyan, a sebastocrator (a high-ranking official), in the 13th century.

Boyana Church offers a unique and immersive experience of Bulgaria's medieval history and artistic tradition. From its stunning frescoes and historical significance to its tranquil grounds and informative tours, the church provides a captivating journey through time. Whether you're an art aficionado, a history buff, or simply looking for a peaceful retreat, Boyana Church offers an enriching and unforgettable visit.

Chapter seven

Savoring local cuisine

Traditional Bulgarian dishes to try

Shopska Salad (Шопска салата)

Shopska Salad is a vibrant and refreshing dish that perfectly reflects the flavors and colors of Bulgaria. Named after the Shopluk area, which spans parts of Bulgaria, Serbia, and North Macedonia, this salad has become a national favorite. It's a simple yet flavorful mix of fresh vegetables, herbs, and tangy cheese, making it a staple at Bulgarian tables, especially during the warmer months.

Key Ingredients

What makes the Shopska Salad so special? It's all about the fresh, high-quality ingredients that come together to make a symphony of flavors.

Tomatoes: Ripe and juicy, the tomatoes form the base of the salad, giving it a sweet and tangy flavor. Cucumbers: Crisp and refreshing, they add a pleasant crunch.

Red or green bell peppers have a mild sweetness and a bright color.

Red Onion: Thinly sliced red onions add a sharp bite and a touch of color.

Feta Cheese (Sirene): The crowning glory of Shopska Salad, Bulgarian feta cheese, known as "sirene," is crumbled generously on top, giving a creamy and salty finish.

Parsley: Freshly chopped parsley adds a burst of herbal flavor.

Olive Oil: A drizzle of high-quality olive oil improves the flavors and brings everything together. Vinegar: A splash of vinegar adds a pleasant acidity that balances the vegetables' sweetness.

Salt and pepper are simple seasonings that improve the natural flavors of the ingredients.

Where to try it

Shopska Salad is ubiquitous in Bulgaria, and you can find it in almost any restaurant, from casual places to fine dining establishments. Here are a few recommendations:

Made in Home is known for its cozy setting and delicious Bulgarian and international dishes. The address is 30A Angel Kanchev Street, Sofia. Website: Made at Home

Moma Bulgarian Food & Wine is a beautiful restaurant that serves traditional Bulgarian cuisine, including a superb Shopska Salad.

Address: 28 Solunska Street, Sofia
Website: Moma Bulgarian Food & Wine

Pod Lipite offers traditional Bulgarian dishes in a historic setting. The Shopska Salad is a must-try.

Address: 1 Elin Pelin Street, Sofia.
Website: Pod Lipite

Serving Suggestions

Shopska Salad is incredibly versatile and can be enjoyed in different ways:

For an appetizer, start your lunch with Shopska Salad to awaken your palate with its fresh and vibrant flavors.

As a Side Dish: Pair it with grilled meats, fish, or other

main foods for a balanced and refreshing accompaniment.

As a Main Course: For a light and healthy meal, enjoy a larger serving of Shopska Salad with some crusty bread on the side.

Photographs

Imagine a beautiful plate of Shopska Salad, with the bright colors of the tomatoes, cucumbers, and peppers contrasting against the white crumbles of feta cheese, all garnished with fresh parsley. The olive oil glistens in the sunlight, inviting you to take a bite. (Here, you would insert a real photograph of the salad to visually entice the reader.)

Practical Information

Preparation Time: Shopska Salad is quick and simple to make, taking about 10–15 minutes. Food storage: Refrigerate leftover salad in an airtight jar for one day. Note that it's best eaten fresh. Nutritional Benefits: This salad is packed with vitamins and minerals, thanks to the fresh vegetables, and offers a good source of protein from the feta cheese.

Shopska Salad is more than just a meal; it's a

celebration of fresh, simple ingredients that come together to create something truly special. Whether you're enjoying it in a busy Sofia restaurant or making it at home, this salad offers a delicious taste of Bulgarian culture.

Banitsa (Баница)

Banitsa is a classic Bulgarian pastry made by layering sheets of filo dough with a mixture of eggs, yogurt, and feta cheese, then baking it until golden and flaky. It's a versatile dish that can be enjoyed at any time of the day, whether for breakfast, a snack, or a festive event. Each bite of Banitsa offers a perfect mix of crispiness from the filo and creamy richness from the cheese filling, making it a comforting and satisfying treat.

Key Ingredients

What makes Banitsa so irresistible? It's all about the simple yet flavorful ingredients:

Filo Dough: thin, flaky pieces of dough that form the pastry's layers.

Crumbled feta cheese (Sirene) adds a tangy and creamy component to the filling.

Eggs: Help bind the mixture and give it a rich texture. Yogurt adds moisture and a slight tang to the filling, improving the overall flavor.

Butter or oil is used to brush the filo layers, resulting in a golden, crispy crust.

Baking soda is sometimes added to the yogurt to make the filling fluffier.

Where to try it

Banitsa is a staple in Bulgarian food, and you can find it in bakeries, cafes, and restaurants across the country. Here are some of the best places in Sofia to try Banitsa: HleBar is a cozy bakery known for its freshly made goods, including delectable bananas.

Address: 10 Tsar Shishman Street, Sofia
Website: HleBar

Shtastlivetsa serves a variety of traditional Bulgarian dishes, including the superb Banitsa.

Address: 27 Vitosha Boulevard, Sofia
Website: Shtastlivetsa

Made in Home is a stylish restaurant that serves a mix

of Bulgarian and international dishes, with Banitsa frequently appearing on the menu.

The address is 30A Angel Kanchev Street, Sofia. Website: Made at Home

Serving Suggestions

Banitsa is incredibly versatile and can be enjoyed in different ways.

Breakfast Delight: Start your day with a slice of warm Banitsa, paired with a cup of coffee or tea. Snack Time: Enjoy Banitsa as a mid-morning or afternoon snack, ideal for curbing hunger between meals.

Festive Treat: Banitsa is often made for special occasions and holidays, such as Christmas and New Year's Eve, sometimes with lucky charms or fortunes baked inside.

Accompaniments: For a light meal, serve Banitsa with a side of Bulgarian yogurt or fresh salad.

Photographs

Imagine a golden-brown Banitsa, fresh out of the oven, with its flaky layers and creamy filling visible through the cracks. The scent of butter and cheese fills the air, inviting you to take a bite. (Here, you would put an actual photograph of Banitsa to visually entice the reader.)

Practical Information

Banitsa is relatively simple to make, with a preparation time of about 30 minutes and a baking time of around 40 minutes.

Storage: If you have leftovers, put Banitsa in an airtight container at room temperature for up to two days or refrigerate for up to five days. Reheat in the oven for the best results.

Nutritional Benefits: Banitsa is rich in protein and calcium from the cheese and eggs, making it a filling and nutritious choice.

Banitsa is more than just a pastry; it's a beloved Bulgarian tradition that brings comfort and joy to anyone who eats it. From its crisp, flaky layers to its creamy, tangy filling, every bite of Banitsa tells a story of Bulgarian culinary history. Whether you're having it in a bustling bakery in Sofia or trying your hand at making it at home, Banitsa offers a delicious and authentic experience that's sure to delight.

Kavarma (Каварма)

Kavarma is a traditional Bulgarian stew that's known for its rich and robust taste. Typically made with tender chunks of pork, onions, peppers, tomatoes, and a blend of spices, kavarma is slow-cooked to perfection. The result is a mouthwatering dish where the meat is incredibly tender and the veggies meld into a flavorful sauce. Kavarma, served hot, usually in a clay pot, is the epitome of Bulgarian comfort food and is perfect for a cozy meal.

Key Ingredients

What makes Kavarma so irresistible? It's all about the rich, hearty ingredients that come together in a medley of flavors:

Pork is the main protein, often cubed and browned to improve its flavor.

Onions add sweetness and depth to the stew. Bell Peppers: Red or green bell peppers add color and a mild sweetness.

Tomatoes: Fresh or canned tomatoes provide flavor and a rich base for the sauce.

Mushrooms are optional, but they add an earthy taste that complements the other ingredients.

Wine: A splash of red or white wine improves the stew's depth and richness.

Paprika: Sweet or smoked paprika adds comfort and a slight smokiness.

Garlic: Fresh garlic cloves add a strong, aromatic quality.

Bay leaves impart a subtle, herbal taste. Herbs: fresh parsley or thyme for garnish. Salt and pepper: simple spices to taste.

Where to try it

Kavarma is a staple in Bulgarian food and can be found in many traditional restaurants. Here are a few of the best spots in Sofia to try Kavarma: Hadjidraganov's Houses is known for its authentic Bulgarian cuisine and rustic atmosphere.

Address: 75 Kozloduy Street, Sofia
Website: Hadjidraganov's Houses

Moma Bulgarian Food & Wine offers a beautiful

setting and a menu full of traditional Bulgarian foods, including kavarma.

Address: 28 Solunska Street, Sofia
Website: Moma Bulgarian Food & Wine

Shtastlivetsa is a popular restaurant that serves a range of Bulgarian classics.

Address: 27 Vitosha Boulevard, Sofia
Website: Shtastlivetsa

Serving Suggestions

Kavarma is a versatile dish that can be enjoyed in different ways.

Kavarma is served as a hearty main course, followed by a side of fresh bread to soak up the delicious sauce. For a full and satisfying meal, pair it with rice, mashed potatoes, or even bulgur.

Garnishes: Sprinkle fresh parsley or thyme on top for a burst of color and taste.

Wine Pairing: To complement the rich flavors of the stew, enjoy it with a glass of Bulgarian red wine, such as Mavrud or Melnik.

Photographs

Imagine a steaming clay pot filled with tender chunks of pork, bright veggies, and a rich, savory sauce. The dish is garnished with fresh parsley, and the flavor of paprika and garlic fills the air. (Here, you would put an actual photograph of Kavarma to visually entice the reader.)

Practical Information

Kavarma takes some time to make, with about 20 minutes of prep time and 1.5 to 2 hours of cooking time for the flavors to fully develop.

Storage: For up to three days, store leftover kavarma in an airtight jar in the refrigerator. Reheat slowly on the stove for best results.

Nutritional Benefits: Kavarma is a protein-rich dish with a beneficial mix of vegetables, making it a hearty and nutritious meal.

Kavarma is more than just a stew; it's a culinary trip into the heart of Bulgarian tradition. From its tender pork and vibrant vegetables to its rich, flavorful sauce, every bite of Kavarma tells a story of comfort and tradition. Whether you're savoring it in a traditional Bulgarian restaurant or trying your hand at making it at home, Kavarma offers a delicious and authentic experience that's sure to please.

The Best Restaurants for Authentic Food

1. Hadjidraganov's Houses

Location: 75 Kozloduy Street, Sofia, Bulgaria.

Traditional Bulgarian foods such as Kavarma, Shopska Salad, and Banitsa are specialties.

Ambiance: Step into Hadjidraganov's houses and be taken back in time. The restaurant is set in a charming complex of restored 19th-century houses, boasting wooden interiors, traditional decor, and a cozy, rustic atmosphere. Each room is uniquely decorated, giving you a sense of Bulgaria's rich cultural history. Price Range: Moderate: Expect to spend around 20–40 BGN per person for a full meal.

Opening hours: Daily from 12 p.m. to 11 p.m. Reservation Information: Reservations are suggested, especially during weekends and holidays. You can book a table by phone or through their website. Dietary Options: Vegetarian options are available, and the restaurant can handle some dietary restrictions upon request.

Hadjidraganov's Houses is more than just a restaurant; it is a cultural event. The restaurant often features live folk music and traditional dance acts, adding to the immersive Bulgarian dining experience. Guest Reviews: Guests rave about the authentic setting, delicious food, and friendly service. Many consider the Kavarma and the lively traditional music to be standout features.

Contact Information:

Phone: +359 2 931 31 48
Website: Hadjidraganov's Houses

2. Moma Bulgarian Food & Wine

Location: 28 Solunska Street, Sofia, Bulgaria.

Specialties: A diverse menu offering traditional Bulgarian dishes such as stuffed peppers, moussaka, and the signature Moma Salad. Ambiance: Moma Bulgarian Food & Wine blends modern elegance with traditional charm. The interior is beautifully decorated with modern touches and traditional Bulgarian elements, creating a warm and inviting atmosphere.

Price Range: Moderate to High: Expect to spend around 30–50 BGN per person for a full meal. Opening hours: Daily from 12 p.m. to 11 p.m. Reservation Information: Reservations are highly suggested, especially for dinner and on weekends. You can book a table through their website or by phone.

Dietary Options: Vegetarian, vegan, and gluten-free options are offered. The staff is knowledgeable and can help accommodate different dietary needs. Cultural Significance: Moma Bulgarian Food & Wine is committed to preserving and promoting Bulgarian culinary traditions. The restaurant's name, "Moma," refers to a young Bulgarian maiden, representing purity and tradition.

Guest Reviews: Guests praise the restaurant for its beautifully presented dishes, excellent wine choices, and exceptional service. The atmosphere is described as both sophisticated and friendly.

Contact Information:

Phone: +359 88 634 34 34
Website: Moma Bulgarian Food & Wine

3. Shtastlivetsa

Location: 27 Vitosha Boulevard, Sofia, Bulgaria. Specialties: A wide range of Bulgarian classics like lamb chops, Gyuvech (vegetable stew), and homemade sweets such as Tikvenik (pumpkin pie).

Ambiance: Located on the bustling Vitosha Boulevard, Shtastlivetsa offers a chic and stylish setting with a mix of traditional and modern decor. The big windows provide a wonderful view of the lively street outside, making it perfect for people-watching.

Price Range: Moderate: Expect to spend around 25–45 BGN per person for a full meal.

Opening Hours: Daily from 11 a.m. to 11 p.m. Reservation Information: Reservations are recommended, especially during peak hours and weekends. You can book a table online or by calling the restaurant.

Dietary choices: The menu includes a variety of vegetarian choices and some gluten-free dishes. The staff is accommodating to dietary tastes and allergies. Cultural Significance: Shtastlivetsa translates to "The Happy One," a perfect name for a place that aims to provide a joyful dining experience. The restaurant's menu is inspired by classic Bulgarian recipes, brought to life with a modern twist.

Guest Reviews: Diners love the vibrant atmosphere, broad food, and attentive service. The restaurant is frequently praised for its creative take on Bulgarian food and its lively, welcoming vibe.

Contact Information:

Phone: +359 2 441 11 11
Website: Shtastlivetsa

Exploring Sofia's culinary landscape is a journey through Bulgaria's rich past and culture. Hadjidraganov's Houses, Moma Bulgarian Food & Wine, and Shtastlivetsa each offer a unique and authentic dining experience that displays the best of Bulgarian cuisine. Whether you're savoring a hearty stew, enjoying live folk music, or indulging in beautifully presented dishes, these places promise a memorable meal. and a lot more of the best places for authentic food in Sofia.

Markets and street food

Street food delights

1. Street Burger

Location: Various food trucks across Sofia are typically found in areas like Vitosha Boulevard and Sofia University.
Popular Stalls and Vendors: Street burger trucks are known for their quality and dependability. Look out for the bright, graffiti-covered trucks with "Street Burger" signs.

Signature Dishes:

Classic Cheeseburger: a juicy beef patty topped with melted cheese, fresh lettuce, tomato, and a spicy special sauce.
Bacon BBQ Burger: Beef patty with crispy bacon, spicy BBQ sauce, and cheddar cheese, served with a side of golden fries.

Operating Hours: Typically, from 11 a.m. to 10 p.m., but hours can change by location.

Ambiance: The environment is lively and casual, with the enticing aroma of grilled burgers filling the air. It's a favorite spot for both locals and tourists looking for a quick, delicious bite.

Burgers range in price from 7 to 12 BGN, making them affordable.

Cultural Significance: Street food like Street Burger reflects Sofia's embrace of international flavors while keeping a local twist. It's a testament to the city's evolving culinary scene.

Tips for Visitors: Try to come during off-peak hours to avoid long lines. Don't forget to grab extra napkins, as these juicy burgers can get messy! Safety and Hygiene: Street Burger trucks are known for their cleanliness and adherence to food safety guidelines. Look for vendors with obvious hygiene certifications.
Photographs: Picture a lively food truck with a line of eager customers, the grill sizzling with fresh patties, and the finished product—a mouthwatering burger oozing with cheese and topped with crisp vegetables.

2. Banitsa Express

Location: Often found near major transportation hubs like Sofia Central Station and Serdika Metro Station. Popular Stalls/Vendors: Banitsa Express kiosks are easily recognizable by their traditional Bulgarian decor and the enticing smell of newly baked pastries.

Signature Dishes:

Classic Banitsa: Flaky filo dough filled with a mixture of eggs, yogurt, and feta cheese, baked to golden perfection.
Spinach Banitsa: A spinach-filled variation that adds a fresh twist to the classic recipe.

Operating Hours: Typically, from 6 a.m. to 8 p.m., making it a wonderful choice for breakfast or a quick snack.

Ambiance: The atmosphere is bustling, especially in the mornings, as travelers and locals stop by for their favorite pastry. The smell of freshly baked bananas is enticing.

Banitsa pieces range in price from 2 to 5 BGN, making them very affordable.

Cultural Significance: Banitsa is a beloved staple in Bulgarian food, and enjoying it from a street vendor is a quintessential local experience.

Tips for Visitors: Go early in the morning for the best bananas. Pair it with a bottle of Ayran (a yogurt-based drink) for a classic Bulgarian breakfast. Safety and Hygiene: Banitsa Express stalls maintain high standards of hygiene, and the pastries are made fresh daily.

Photographs: Imagine a bustling kiosk with trays of golden bananas, the crispy layers visible, and steam rising from newly baked batches as customers eagerly line up for their favorite treat.

Bustling Markets

1. Central Market Hall (Централни хали)

Location: Maria Luiza Blvd. 25, Sofia, Bulgaria
Popular Stalls and Vendors: The market features a wide range of vendors selling everything from fresh fruit to artisanal cheeses and traditional Bulgarian sweets.

Signature Dishes:

Kebapche: grilled minced meat skewers, often eaten with a side of lyutenitsa (a red pepper and tomato relish).
Baklava is a sweet, flaky pastry layered with nuts and honey syrup, perfect for dessert.

Operating Hours: Monday to Saturday from 7 AM to 7 PM; Sunday from 8 AM to 6 PM.

Ambiance: The Central Market Hall is vibrant and bustling, with the sounds of vendors calling out their wares and the smell of fresh food filling the air. The building itself is a beautiful piece of design with historical charm.

Price range: moderate, with items available for a wide range of budgets.

Cultural Significance: The market hall has been a key part of Sofia's trade and daily life since its opening in 1911. It's a place where tradition meets the present, giving a taste of Bulgarian heritage.

Tips for Visitors: Take your time to explore all three floors of the market. Don't be afraid to haggle a bit for a better price on things.

Safety and Hygiene: The market is well-regulated, with sellers adhering to hygiene standards. However, always wash fresh food before consumption. Photographs: Visualize a bustling market hall with vendors showcasing bright displays of fruits, vegetables, spices, and traditional Bulgarian goods. The historic building adds a unique charm to the lively atmosphere.

2. Women's Market (Женски пазар)

Location: Stefan Stambolov Blvd., Sofia, Bulgaria Popular Stalls and Vendors: Known for its wide range of fresh produce, spices, and traditional foods. You can also find household items and clothes.

Signature Dishes:

Lyutenitsa, a traditional Bulgarian spread made from tomatoes and peppers, is great for spreading on bread or accompanying meats.

Sirene is a Bulgarian white cheese, similar to feta, which is a staple in many local recipes.

Operating Hours: Daily from 7 a.m. to 7 p.m.

Ambiance: The Women's Market is lively and eclectic, giving a true slice of local life. It's a bit more hectic than the Central Market Hall, but full of character and charm.

Price Range: Very cheap, making it a favorite among locals for everyday shopping.

Cultural Significance: Historically, the market has been a key spot for local trade, reflecting Sofia's daily life and cultural diversity.

Tips for Visitors: Arrive early in the day for the freshest food. Keep an eye on your things, as the market can get crowded.

Safety and Hygiene: While the market is usually safe, it's always beneficial to practice typical market precautions. Look for sellers with clean and well-organized stalls.

Photographs: Imagine a lively outdoor market with stalls overflowing with colorful fruits, vegetables, spices, and handmade goods. The energy is palpable, with locals haggling and vendors showcasing their best goods.

Exploring Sofia's street food and markets is like stepping into the city's culinary heart. These experiences offer a taste of Sofia's rich culture and active life, from the mouthwatering burgers of Street Burger to the traditional pastries at Banitsa Express to the historic charm of the Central Market Hall to the bustling atmosphere of the Women's Market.

Vegetarian and vegan options

Vegetarian Options

1. Sunmoon (Слънце Луна)

Location: 15 Aksakov Street, Sofia, Bulgaria. Menu Highlights: Sunmoon is a bakery and vegetarian diner known for its wholesome and organic ingredients. The menu features a variety of salads, soups, and baked goods that celebrate fresh, seasonal food.

Specialty Dishes:

Vegetarian Moussaka: A delicious take on the classic dish, made with layers of potatoes, zucchini, and eggplant, topped with a creamy béchamel sauce. Sunmoon Salad: A hearty salad with mixed greens, roasted veggies, nuts, and seeds, drizzled with a tangy vinaigrette.

Ambiance: Sunmoon offers a cozy and rustic setting with wooden furnishings and a warm, inviting vibe. The smell of freshly baked bread and pastries fills the air, adding to the homey feel.

Price Range: Moderate: Expect to spend around 15–25 BGN per person for a meal.

Opening Hours: Daily from 8 a.m. to 10 p.m.

Reservation Information: Reservations are suggested, especially on weekends. You can book a place by phone or through their website.

Guest Reviews: Guests love the fresh and flavorful dishes, friendly staff, and charming setting. Many highlight the bakery items and the creative vegetarian choices.

Dietary Certifications: The restaurant uses organic and locally sourced ingredients, and many meals are gluten-free.

Contact Information:

Phone: +359 88 545 4545
Website: Sunmoon

2. Kring

Location: 9 Tsar Simeon Street, Sofia, Bulgaria.
Menu Highlights: Kring is a vegetarian restaurant that focuses on healthy and balanced meals inspired by different international cuisines. The menu includes a mix of traditional Bulgarian dishes and world favorites.

Specialty Dishes:

Vegetarian Sarmi: Grape leaves stuffed with rice, herbs, and veggies, served with a tangy yogurt sauce. Kring Burger: A filling veggie burger made with a chickpea patty, fresh veggies, and a special house sauce. Ambiance: Kring has a bright and modern atmosphere, as well as a relaxed and friendly setting. The decor is simple yet stylish, making it a perfect spot for a casual meal.

Price Range: Affordable to Moderate: Expect to spend around 10–20 BGN per person for a meal. Opening Hours: Monday to Saturday from 11 a.m. to 9 p.m.; closed on Sundays.

Reservation Information: Reservations are not normally necessary but can be made by phone for larger groups.

Guest Reviews: Diners enjoy the diverse menu, delicious flavors, and welcoming environment. The friendly service and healthy choices are frequently praised.

Dietary Certifications: Kring offers many gluten-free and vegan choices, clearly marked on the menu.

Contact Information:

Phone: +359 2 987 8787
Website: Kring

Vegan Options

1. Edgy Veggy

Location: 21 Ivan Denkoglu Street, Sofia, Bulgaria.
Menu Highlights: Edgy Veggy is a trendy vegan restaurant that offers a wide range of plant-based recipes, from comfort foods to healthy eats. The menu includes everything from burgers and wraps to smoothies and sweets.

Specialty Dishes:

Vegan Burger: A delicious burger made with homemade plant-based meat, fresh veggies, and a special vegan sauce, served with a side of sweet potato fries.

Raw Zucchini Pasta: spiralized zucchini noodles with a creamy avocado pesto sauce, cherry tomatoes, and pine nuts.

Ambiance: Edgy Veggy has a hip and bright atmosphere, with modern decor and a lively vibe. It's a popular spot for both lunch and dinner, drawing a diverse crowd.

Price Range: Moderate: Expect to spend around 20–30 BGN per person for a meal.

Opening Hours: Monday to Friday from 11 a.m. to 10 p.m.; Saturday and Sunday from 12 p.m. to 10 p.m.

Reservation Information: Reservations are suggested for dinner and weekends. You can book a place by phone or through their website.

Guest Reviews: Guests rave about the innovative and tasty vegan dishes, friendly service, and cool environment. The burgers and raw dishes are extremely popular.

Dietary Certifications: The restaurant is totally vegan, and many dishes are also gluten-free and raw, clearly marked on the menu.

Contact Information:

Phone: +359 89 765 4321
Website: Edgy Veggy

2. Soul Kitchen

Location: 13 Tsar Asen Street, Sofia, Bulgaria.
Menu Highlights: Soul Kitchen is a vegan and raw food diner known for its creative and beautifully presented dishes. The menu offers a mix of raw, gluten-free, and cooked vegan options, focused on high-quality, organic ingredients.

Specialty Dishes:

Raw Lasagna: Layers of zucchini, cashew cheese, spinach, and tomato sauce, served with a side salad. Vegan Tacos: Soft tacos stuffed with spiced jackfruit, avocado, and fresh salsa, topped with a tangy vegan sour cream.

Ambiance: Soul Kitchen has a cozy and eclectic atmosphere with a warm, welcoming feel. The decor is a mix of rustic and modern, creating a unique and welcoming atmosphere.

Price Range: Moderate to High: Expect to spend around 25–35 BGN per person for a meal. Opening hours: daily from 12 p.m. to 10 p.m. Reservation Information: Reservations are suggested, especially for dinner. You can book a place by phone or through their website.

Guest Reviews: Diners love the innovative and delicious vegan dishes, the charming setting, and the attentive service. Raw lasagna and vegan desserts are often emphasized.

Dietary Certifications: The restaurant is totally vegan and offers a variety of gluten-free and raw choices, clearly marked on the menu.

Contact Information:

Phone: +359 88 123 4567
Website: Soul Kitchen

Exploring Sofia's vegetarian and vegan culinary scene is a delightful journey into creativity and taste. Sunmoon and Kring offer hearty and wholesome vegetarian options, while Edgy Veggy and Soul Kitchen provide innovative and delectable vegan meals. Each restaurant offers a unique dining experience that showcases the best of plant-based cuisine in Sofia.

Chapter eight

Nightlife and entertainment

The Best Bars and Clubs

1. Sense Hotel Rooftop Bar

Location: 16 Tsar Osvoboditel Blvd., Sofia, Bulgaria
Ambiance: Imagine sipping a cocktail while looking out over the sparkling city lights. The Sense Hotel Rooftop Bar offers a chic and sophisticated setting with panoramic views of Sofia. The stylish decor, comfortable seating, and ambient lighting make it a wonderful spot for a romantic evening or a classy night out with friends.

Signature Drinks:

Basil Smash: A refreshing mix of gin, fresh basil, lemon juice, and simple syrup.

Sofia Sunset: A vibrant cocktail with vodka, orange juice, cranberry juice, and a splash of grenadine.

Price Range: Higher-end: Expect to spend around 20–30 BGN per drink.

Opening Hours: Daily from 6 p.m. to 2 a.m.
Reservation Information: Reservations are suggested, especially for the best seats with a view. You can book a table by phone or through the hotel's website.
Guest Reviews: Guests rave about the breathtaking views, excellent service, and perfectly crafted cocktails. It's a top choice for those looking to enjoy a stylish night out in Sofia.

Contact Information:

Phone: +359 2 446 22 00
Website: Sense Hotel Rooftop Bar

2. The Cocktail Bar

Location: 5 Tsar Shishman Street, Sofia, Bulgaria.
Ambiance: Tucked away in a cozy spot, The Cocktail Bar is a hidden gem with a warm and inviting environment. The bar's eclectic decor, dim lighting, and intimate setting make the perfect backdrop for enjoying a creative cocktail or two.

Signature Drinks:

Old Fashioned: A classic drink made with bourbon, bitters, sugar, and a twist of orange peel.
Lavender Martini: A delicious mix of gin, lavender syrup, lemon juice, and a touch of honey.
Price Range: Moderate: Expect to spend around 10–20 BGN per drink.

Opening Hours: Monday to Saturday from 5 PM to 1 AM; closed on Sundays.

Reservation Information: Reservations are not normally required, but they can get crowded on weekends. Arriving early ensures you get a favorable place.
Guest Reviews: Patrons love the creative drinks, friendly bartenders, and relaxed vibe. The bar's unique drinks and cozy setting make it a favorite among locals and tourists alike.

Contact Information:

Phone: +359 88 888 8888
Website: The Cocktail Bar
Best Clubs

1. Yalta Club

Location: 20 Tsar Osvoboditel Blvd., Sofia, Bulgaria
Ambiance: Yalta Club is Sofia's premier nightclub, known for its electrifying atmosphere and top-notch DJs. With a state-of-the-art sound system and a stylish, modern interior, this club is the go-to destination for electronic dance music fans.

Music Style: Electronic dance music (EDM), house, techno
Price Range: Moderate to High: Entry fees vary from 20 to 40 BGN, depending on the event.
Opening Hours: Friday and Saturday from 11 p.m. to 6 a.m.

Reservation Information: Booking a table or VIP area is suggested for the best experience. You can book online or by phone.

Guest Reviews: Partygoers praise Yalta Club for its incredible music, energetic crowd, and top-tier DJ acts. It's a must-visit for anyone looking to dance the night away in Sofia.

Contact Information:

Phone: +359 2 987 27 27
Website: Yalta Club

2. Club Terminal 1

Location: 1 Angel Kanchev Street, Sofia, Bulgaria.
Ambiance: Club Terminal 1 offers a raw, industrial-chic feel with its exposed brick walls and edgy decor. The club is known for its diverse music lineup and vibrant atmosphere, making it a hotspot for a wide range of music fans.

Music Style: Rock, punk, alternative, electronic
Price Range: Moderate entry fees range from 10 to 30 BGN, depending on the event.
Opening Hours: Wednesday to Saturday from 10 p.m. to 5 a.m.

Reservation Information: Reservations are not usually needed, but it's a good idea to check the event schedule and arrive early for popular shows.
Guest Reviews: Guests love the club's eclectic music selection, energetic crowd, and unique setting. It's a favorite for those looking to enjoy live music and DJ sets in a lively setting.

Contact Information:

Phone: +359 88 888 8889
Website: Club Terminal 1

Sofia's nightlife offers a diverse and exciting array of bars and clubs that cater to all tastes and preferences. From the elegant rooftop views at Sense Hotel Rooftop Bar to the creative drinks at The Cocktail Bar, and from the pulsating beats at Yalta Club to the eclectic sounds at Club Terminal 1, there's something for everyone.

Venues for live music

1. Sofia Live Club

Location: NDK (National Palace of Culture), Bldg. A3, Bulgaria Square, Sofia, Bulgaria
Ambiance: Picture this: a sleek, modern interior with cozy seating, a roomy dance floor, and state-of-the-art acoustics. Sofia Live Club is the go-to place for live music fans, providing an intimate yet electrifying atmosphere where you can immerse yourself in the music.
Music Style: The club offers a variety of genres, from jazz and blues to rock and pop. It's a hub for both local talent and foreign artists.

Signature Events:

Jazz Evenings: Featuring some of the area's best jazz musicians.
Rock Nights are high-energy shows that will have you on your feet all night long.

Price Range: Moderate Entry fees usually range from 10 to 30 BGN, depending on the event.
Opening Hours: Thursday to Saturday from 9 p.m. to 4 a.m.

Reservation Information: Reservations are suggested, especially for popular events. You can book a table online or by phone.

Guest Reviews: Visitors praise the club's fantastic acoustics, wide lineup, and friendly staff. The venue's intimate setting makes it a favorite for music fans who want to be close to the action.

Contact Information:

Phone: +359 88 666 7777
Website: Sofia Live Club

2. Swingin' Hall

Location: 8A Pozitano Street, Sofia, Bulgaria
Ambiance: Swingin' Hall is a lively and friendly venue known for its eclectic decor and energetic vibe. The mood is casual and fun, making it a wonderful place to unwind and enjoy live music with friends. Music Style: The venue is famous for its rock and blues nights but also holds jazz, funk, and even karaoke events.

Signature Events:

Blues Mondays: Start your week with soulful blues concerts.
Rock Fridays are high-octane rock shows that draw a passionate crowd.

Price Range: Affordable to Moderate: Entry fees range from 5 to 20 BGN, making it affordable for everyone. Opening Hours: Monday to Saturday from 9 p.m. to 3 a.m.; closed on Sundays.

Reservation Information: No reservations are required, but it's a good idea to arrive early to get a good spot, especially on weekends.

Guest Reviews: Patrons love the laid-back atmosphere, diverse music choices, and reasonable prices. Swingin'

Hall's friendly crowd and lively acts make it a standout in Sofia's music scene.

Contact Information:

Phone: +359 88 123 4567

Website: Swingin' Hall

3. Club Mixtape 5

Location: NDK Underpass, Sofia, Bulgaria
Ambiance: Club Mixtape 5 boasts a trendy, urban feel with its industrial-chic decor and vibrant energy. The venue is spacious, with plenty of room for dancing and a fantastic sound system that brings every show to life. Music Style: A mix of everything, from dance and hip-hop to indie and alternative rock. It's the place to find new artists and enjoy a wide range of musical styles.

Signature Events:

Indie Nights: A showcase of up-and-coming indie acts. Electronic Sessions: Featuring top DJs and electronic music acts.

Entry fees usually range from 10 to 30 BGN. Price Range: Moderate.

Opening Hours: Friday and Saturday from 10 p.m. to 5 a.m.

Reservation Information: Reservations are not usually required, but it's best to check the event schedule and get tickets in advance for popular shows.

Guest Reviews: Visitors enjoy the club's diverse music lineup, energetic setting, and excellent acoustics. Club Mixtape 5 is a favorite for those looking to experience Sofia's cutting-edge music scene.

Contact Information:

Phone: +359 87 765 4321
Website: Club Mixtape 5

4. Terminal 1

Location: 1 Angel Kanchev Street, Sofia, Bulgaria.
Ambiance: Terminal 1 offers a raw, industrial-chic feel with exposed brick walls and edgy decor. The club is known for its diverse music lineup and vibrant atmosphere, making it a hotspot for a wide range of music fans.

Music Style: Rock, indie, alternative, electronic Terminal 1 gets it all. It's the perfect venue for those who value variety and high-energy performances.

Signature Events:

Rock Wednesdays: mid-week rock sessions that draw a committed crowd.

Electronic Saturdays: Dance the night away with top electronic music acts.

Entry fees range from 10 to 30 BGN; the price range is moderate.
Opening Hours: Wednesday to Saturday from 10 p.m. to 5 a.m.

Reservation Information: Reservations are not usually needed, but it's a good idea to check the event schedule and arrive early for popular shows. Guest Reviews: Guests love the club's eclectic music selection, energetic crowd, and unique setting. It's a favorite for those looking to enjoy live music and DJ sets in a lively setting.

Contact Information:

Phone: +359 88 765 4321
Website: Terminal 1

Sofia's live music venues offer a rich and diverse scene that caters to all musical styles. From the intimate, jazz-infused ambiance of Sofia Live Club to the high-energy rock nights at Swingin' Hall, and from the varied sounds of Club Mixtape 5 to the dynamic vibe of Terminal 1, there's something for everyone.

Theatrical Performances and Cultural Events

Theatrical Performances

National Theatre Ivan Vazov

When it comes to theatrical events in Sofia, the National Theatre Ivan Vazov is the crown jewel. Located in the heart of the city, this grand building is an architectural marvel and a cultural treasure. The theater presents a diverse repertoire, from classical Bulgarian plays to contemporary international works. What to Expect: The performances here are top-notch, featuring some of Bulgaria's best actors and directors.

Whether it's an intense drama or a light-hearted comedy, you're in for a treat.

Pro Tip: Check the theater's schedule in advance and book your tickets early, especially for famous shows. Imagine sitting in this ancient theater's plush red seats, the lights dimming as the curtain rises. The anticipation builds, and for the next few hours, you're taken to another world. It's an event that stays with you long after the final bow.

Sofia Opera and Ballet

For lovers of opera and ballet, the Sofia Opera and Ballet offers performances that match the best in Europe. From famous operas by Verdi and Puccini to stunning ballets like Swan Lake and The Nutcracker, there's something to captivate everyone. What to Expect: Exceptional performances with elaborate costumes, amazing set designs, and powerful music.

Pro Tip: Even if you're not a big opera or ballet fan, experiencing a performance here is worth it just for the sheer artistry and grandeur.

Imagine yourself watching a breathtaking ballet, with the dancers moving with grace and accuracy. The music swells, and you find yourself completely absorbed in the beauty of the performance. It's times like these that make travel so magical.

Sfumato Theatre Laboratory

If you're interested in avant-garde and experimental theater, Sfumato Theatre Laboratory is the place to go. This innovative theater pushes the limits of traditional performances, giving thought-provoking and often unconventional productions.

What to Expect: Bold, experimental performances that challenge the norms and ask you to think deeply. Pro Tip: Keep an open mind and be prepared for a unique theater experience that might be different from anything you've seen before.

Cultural Events

Sofia Film Fest

The Sofia Film Fest is one of Sofia's most anticipated cultural events. Held annually in March, this festival presents a diverse selection of films from around the world, including Bulgarian cinema. What to Expect: screenings of feature films, documentaries, and short films, along with Q&A sessions with directors and stars. Pro Tip: Purchase a festival pass if you plan on watching multiple flicks. It's a wonderful way to immerse yourself in the festival mood.

Imagine sitting in a packed cinema with the lights dimming as a highly anticipated film starts. There's a sense of excitement in the air, and your part of a group of film lovers enjoying the same cinematic journey. It's a wonderful way to connect with others and share in the magic of movies.

Sofia Music Week

Sofia Music Weeks is an international music event held every spring, celebrating a wide range of musical genres, from classical and jazz to folk and contemporary music. It's a must-visit for any music lover.

What to Expect: Concerts by famous musicians and orchestras, as well as performances by emerging acts. Pro Tip: Check the festival program and attend a range of performances to experience the full spectrum of musical offerings.

Imagine yourself at an outdoor show, with the sun setting behind the stage while a symphony orchestra fills the air with beautiful music. The atmosphere is electric, and you feel a deep connection to the music and the people around you. It's an unforgettable event.

Sofia Pride

Sofia Pride, held annually in June, is a vibrant celebration of love, diversity, and equality. It includes a parade, concerts, and different cultural events, promoting LGBTQ+ rights and visibility.

What to Expect: A colorful parade through the streets of Sofia, followed by acts, speeches, and festivities.

Pro Tip: Join the parties and show your support. It's a joyful and inclusive event that accepts everyone. Imagine walking in the parade, surrounded by people dressed in bright colors, waving rainbow flags, and sharing smiles. The sense of community and solidarity is obvious, and your part of a movement that celebrates love and acceptance. It's a heartwarming event.

Local festivals and traditions

Surva Festival

The Surva Festival, held in the nearby town of Pernik but easily reachable from Sofia, is an international festival of masquerade games. It's one of the most famous and unique events in Bulgaria, showcasing traditional Bulgarian masks and costumes. What to Expect: Parades of people dressed in intricate masks and costumes, performing traditional dances and routines to drive away evil spirits. Pro Tip: Visit the festival's workshops to learn about the masks' background and making. It's a fascinating look into Bulgarian folklore.

Imagine watching a parade of people in elaborate costumes with the sound of bells and drums filling the air. The energy is infectious, and you find yourself captivated by the rich cultural heritage on display. It's an event like no other.

Rose Festival

Bulgaria is famous for its roses, and the Rose Festival in Kazanlak, a short trip from Sofia, is a beautiful celebration of this history. Held in June, the event features a rose-picking ritual, parades, and a beauty pageant.
What to Expect: Fields of blooming roses, traditional

music and dancing, and the crowning of the Rose Queen.

Pro Tip: Plan a day trip from Sofia to Kazanlak to enjoy this fragrant and colorful festival. Imagine walking through fields of roses, the air heavy with their sweet smell. You watch the locals perform traditional dances, their colorful outfits swirling in the sunlight. It's a feast for the senses, as well as a celebration of Bulgaria's flower pride.

Sofia's theatrical shows and cultural events offer a rich tapestry of experiences that reflect the city's dynamic spirit. Whether you're captivated by a dramatic play, moved by an opera, or immersed in a vibrant festival, Sofia's culture scene has something to offer everyone.

Seasonal festivals and celebrations

Throughout the year, it hosts a variety of seasonal festivals and celebrations that showcase its rich culture, customs, and joyous spirit. Whether you're a fan of music, dance, food, or tradition, there's something here for everyone.

Spring: Rebirth and Renewal

Baba Marta (March 1st) Spring in Bulgaria starts with Baba Marta, a unique celebration that marks the end of winter and the arrival of spring. Bulgarians share martenitsi, which are red and white yarn ornaments that symbolize health and happiness.

What to Expect: People wear martenitsi on their wrists or pinned to their clothes until they see the first stork or flower, then tie them to a tree. Fun Fact: The red and white colors represent purity and life.

Concider walking through Sofia in early March, seeing everyone adorned with these charming red and white gifts. It's a visual reminder of the common hope for warmer, brighter days ahead.

International Women's Day (March 8th) International Women's Day is marked with great enthusiasm in Sofia. It's a day to celebrate women's achievements and show appreciation for the important women in one's life.

What to Expect: Flowers are given to mothers, wives, sisters, and friends. There are also special events and shows throughout the city.

Pro Tip: Join in by giving flowers to the women you meet—it's a lovely way to participate in this heartfelt tradition.

Imagine yourself buying a bouquet from a local flower shop. The streets are filled with people holding flowers and smiling. It's a beautiful celebration of respect and thanks.

Summer: sun and festivities

Sofia Music Weeks (end of May–June) Sofia Music Weeks is an international music event that brings together a wide range of musical genres, from classical and jazz to folk and contemporary music. What to Expect: Concerts, recitals, and performances by famous musicians and orchestras from around the world.

Pro Tip: Check the festival program and book tickets in advance for the most popular shows. Imagine a warm summer evening, sitting in an open-air setting, the air filled with the enchanting sounds of a live orchestra. It's a unique way to spend a summer night.

Sofia Pride (June) Sofia Pride is a vibrant celebration of love, variety, and equality. It includes a parade, concerts, and different cultural events, promoting LGBTQ+ rights and visibility.

What to Expect: A colorful parade through the streets of Sofia, followed by acts, speeches, and festivities. Pro Tip: Wear something colorful and join the parade to show your support and unity.

Picture the streets filled with rainbow flags, smiling faces, and a joyous mood. It's a powerful and uplifting celebration that welcomes everyone.

Autumn, Harvest, and Heritage

Bulgarian Independence Day (September 22nd) This national holiday honors Bulgaria's independence from the Ottoman Empire in 1908. It's a day of national pride and thought.

What to Expect: Official ceremonies, parades, and cultural events. Many museums and historical sites offer free admission.

Pro Tip: Visit the historical landmarks in Sofia to deepen your understanding of Bulgaria's rich past.

Imagine standing in front of the Alexander Nevsky Cathedral, listening to patriotic songs and talks, and feeling a deep sense of connection to Bulgaria's past and present.

Sofia International Film Festival (March; also extended events in autumn) While mainly held in March, this renowned film festival often has extended events in the autumn, showcasing a diverse range of films from around the world.

What to Expect: screenings of feature films, documentaries, and short films, along with Q&A sessions with directors and stars.

Pro Tip: Get a festival pass to enjoy a wide range of films and immerse yourself in the cinematic culture. Picture yourself in a cozy theater, the lights dimming as an eagerly anticipated film starts. The crowd around you shares your excitement, creating a sense of community through film.

Winter: Warmth and Wonder

Christmas Markets (December) Sofia's Christmas markets are magical places where you can enjoy festive treats, buy handmade gifts, and soak up the holiday spirit.

What to expect: Stalls selling crafts, gifts, and delicious foods like grilled sausages, mulled wine, and sweets. Pro Tip: Visit the market in front of the National Palace of Culture for a particularly festive mood. Imagine strolling through a bustling market, with the smell of pine and spices in the air and lights twinkling above. It's a heartwarming way to get into the holiday mood.

The Surva Festival (end of January) Although it is held in the nearby town of Pernik, the Surva Festival is easily accessible from Sofia and is one of Bulgaria's most unique winter celebrations. It's a worldwide festival of masquerade games.

What to Expect: Parades of people dressed in elaborate masks and costumes, performing traditional dances and practices to drive away evil spirits. Pro Tip: Take a day trip from Sofia to experience this fascinating event.

watching the parades, the sound of bells and drums filling the air, and being part of a centuries-old ritual. It's a cultural experience like no other.

Sofia's seasonal festivals and celebrations offer a wonderful glimpse into the city's vibrant culture and customs. Whether you're coming in the spring, summer, autumn, or winter, there's always something exciting happening.

Chapter nine

Shopping in Sofia

Trendy Boutiques and Fashion Stores

MUSE Shop

Located in the heart of Sofia, MUSE Shop is a must-visit for fashion fans. This chic boutique features a curated range of contemporary clothing and accessories from both Bulgarian and foreign designers. The shop is known for its stylish and elegant atmosphere, making it a perfect spot to find unique and trendy pieces.

How to get there:

MUSE Shop is conveniently located on Vitosha Boulevard, Sofia's main shopping street. You can easily get there by taking the metro to Serdika Station, then going a short distance.

What to buy:

Stylish Dresses: From casual day dresses to elegant evening gowns, MUSE Shop offers a variety of choices that are perfect for any occasion. Trendy Tops: Find the latest in fashion tops, including blouses, shirts, and crop tops that are both fashionable and comfy.

Unique Accessories: Add a touch of Sofia's fashion flair to your clothing with accessories like statement jewelry, scarves, and handbags.

Outerwear: Browse through their collection of stylish coats and jackets that blend fashion and function. Imagine walking down Vitosha Boulevard, the city's main shopping street, and stepping into the MUSE Shop. You're met by friendly staff and a beautifully arranged store filled with fashionable pieces that make your heart race. The ambiance is sophisticated, and each item feels like it has been picked with care.

Rara Avis

Rara Avis is another boutique to keep an eye out for. Known for its avant-garde and bold fashion statements, this store offers clothing that stands out from the crowd. The designs at Rara Avis are not for the faint-hearted but for those who love to make a statement and accept their individuality.

How to get there:

Rara Avis is found near the National Palace of Culture. You can train to the National Palace of Culture (NDK) Station and walk a few blocks.

What to buy:

Statement Dresses: From dramatic evening gowns to quirky day dresses, Rara Avis offers pieces that are ideal for making a bold fashion statement. Their outerwear line includes unique coats and jackets with intricate designs and high-quality fabrics. Artistic Accessories: Look for bold jewelry, unique handbags, and other accessories that add an extra flair to any outfit.

Custom Pieces: Rara Avis also offers custom-designed clothes for those who want something truly unique. Picture yourself trying on a beautiful dress that makes you feel like a runway model. The store's unique designs are ideal for those who love to push fashion boundaries and express their individuality. The ambiance at Rara Avis is creative and inspiring, encouraging you to try out new styles.

Hip Hip Atelier

Hip Hip Atelier is a boutique that honors creativity and individuality. This shop offers a range of clothing and accessories created by local artists and designers, making it a fantastic place to discover one-of-a-kind pieces.

How to get there:

Located in the busy Shishman Street area, Hip Hip Atelier can be reached by taking the metro to Sofia University Station and then walking a few minutes.

What to buy:

Artistic Apparel: Find T-shirts, dresses, and skirts showing original artwork by Bulgarian artists. Handcrafted Accessories: Discover unique jewelry, bags, and hats that showcase local workmanship.

Limited Editions: Many items are made in limited quantities, ensuring you'll have something unique. Imagine walking through Shishman Street, known for its artistic vibe, and stepping into Hip Hip Atelier. The boutique feels like a gallery, with each piece telling a story and reflecting the spirit of Sofia's vibrant artistic community.

Plus Zero Concept Store

For those who love minimalist yet stylish clothes, Plus Zero Concept Store is a must-visit. This boutique focuses on clean lines, neutral colors, and high-quality materials, creating pieces that are both timeless and contemporary.

How to get there:

The Plus Zero Concept Store is situated in the city's heart, near the Vitosha Boulevard area. Take the train to Serdika Station and enjoy a short walk to the store.

What to buy:

Minimalist Clothing: Shop for dresses, tops, and trousers that epitomize minimalist grace. Eco-Friendly Fashion: The store also offers sustainable fashion options, which is beneficial for environmentally conscious shoppers.

Accessories: Find understated jewelry, sleek bags, and stylish shoes that match the minimalist aesthetic. Imagine entering the Plus Zero Concept Store, where the mood is calm and serene. Each item is thoughtfully displayed, making it easy to find pieces that will easily integrate into your wardrobe.

Local Crafts and Souvenirs

Sofia is a treasure trove of local crafts and souvenirs that show the rich cultural heritage of Bulgaria. Whether you're looking for a unique memento of your trip or a special gift for someone back home, Sofia offers a variety of choices to choose from. Here are some top spots to find the perfect souvenir and engage yourself in the local culture.

Central Market Hall (Tsentralni Hali)

Located in the city center, the Central Market Hall is a bustling market where you can find a range of local crafts, foods, and souvenirs. This historic building is not only a shopping center but also an architectural gem worth visiting.

How to get there:

Take the train to Serdika Station, and the market is just a short walk away. The house itself is difficult to miss with its beautiful facade.

What to buy:

Handmade Pottery: Look for beautifully crafted ceramic bowls, plates, and vases that feature traditional Bulgarian designs.

Traditional Bulgarian needlework: From tablecloths and pillowcases to clothes and accessories, the intricate needlework is a true testament to Bulgarian craftsmanship.

Rose Oil Products: Bulgaria is famous for its rose oil, and you can find everything from pure rose oil to rose-scented soaps, lotions, and perfumes. These make for luxurious gifts, especially Bulgarian ones.

wandering through the aisles of the Central Market Hall, your senses delighted by the colors, textures, and scents. You pick up a beautifully stitched tablecloth, knowing it will remind you of Sofia every time you see it.

Sofia Flea Market

For unique and one-of-a-kind gifts, the Sofia Flea Market is a wonderful place to explore. Here, you can find vintage things, antiques, and handmade crafts that tell a story and carry a bit of history.

How to get there:

The market is held near Alexander Nevsky Cathedral. Take the metro to Serdika Station and walk to the church.

What to buy:

Antique Jewelry: Discover rings, necklaces, and brooches with detailed patterns and a sense of history. Vintage Postcards: These make for charming and affordable souvenirs that catch Sofia's historical and cultural essence.

Traditional Bulgarian Crafts: Look for handmade wooden items, traditional musical instruments, and other crafts that showcase Bulgarian history. Imagine looking through a stall of vintage postcards, each one a little piece of history. You find one with a beautiful old picture of Sofia, perfect for framing and adding a nostalgic touch to your home.

Zhenski Pazar (a women's market)

Zhenski Pazar, or Women's Market, is one of the oldest and most lively markets in Sofia. It's a wonderful place to find fresh produce, spices, and a variety of traditional Bulgarian goods.

How to get there:

Take the metro to Serdika Station and then walk towards the market area. It's a short walk from the city center.

What to buy:

Local Spices and Herbs: Bring home the flavors of Bulgaria with a selection of spices and herbs widely used in Bulgarian cuisine.

Handmade Soaps and Candles: These make for lovely gifts and are often infused with local smells like lavender and rose.
Traditional Bulgarian Cheese and Honey: If you have the means to transport them, these culinary delights are a taste of Bulgaria you can share with friends and family.

Think yourself navigating the bustling lanes of Zhenski Pazar, the air filled with fresh herb and spice scents. You taste some locally made cheese and decide to take some home, savoring the idea of sharing a piece of Sofia with your loved ones.

Vitosha Boulevard

While Vitosha Boulevard is known for its trendy boutiques and fashion stores, it also has several shops that offer high-quality gifts and local crafts.

How to get there: Vitosha Boulevard is centrally placed and easily accessible by metro, with Serdika Station being the closest stop.

What to buy:

Artisanal Chocolates and Sweets: Indulge in locally made chocolates and traditional Bulgarian sweets, such as lokum (a Turkish treat).

Bulgarian Wine: Bulgaria has a rich winemaking history, and a bottle of local wine makes for an elegant souvenir.

Handmade Jewelry: Find unique pieces crafted by local artisans that show Bulgarian style and craftsmanship. Imagine strolling down Vitosha Boulevard, window shopping, and popping into a charming store to buy a bottle of fine Bulgarian wine. Each sip later will bring back thoughts of your time in Sofia.

Vitosha Mountain Craft Stalls

If you're planning a trip to Vitosha Mountain, don't miss the craft stalls near the famous tourist spots. These stalls offer a range of handmade goods that make perfect souvenirs.

How to get there:

You can take a bus or a short cab ride to Vitosha Mountain from Sofia City Center. The stalls are usually located near the major hiking trails and picnic areas.

What to buy:

Hand-knitted Woolens: Pick up cozy hats, scarves, and mittens made from locally found wool. Wooden Carvings: Look for beautifully made wooden spoons, bowls, and decorative items. Traditional Dolls: These handmade dolls dressed in traditional Bulgarian attire make for charming keepsakes.

Taking a break from hiking to browse the craft stalls and finding a hand-knitted scarf that will keep you warm back home while reminding you of your adventures on Vitosha Mountain.

Flea Markets and Antique Shops

For those who love the thrill of discovering hidden gems, Sofia's flea markets and antique shops are excellent for finding unique treasures. These spots offer a glimpse into Bulgaria's past, with a variety of vintage and antique things that tell stories of a bygone era.

Bitaka Flea Market

Bitaka Flea Market is a local favorite for finding antiques, vintage goods, and collectibles. It's a vibrant market where you can browse through a variety of stalls, each brimming with possible treasures.

How to get there:

The market is located near Sofia's Mall. Take the metro to Opalchenska Station and walk a short distance to reach the market.

What to buy:

Antique Jewelry: Look for beautifully crafted pieces from different times, including rings, necklaces, and brooches.

Vintage Toys: Discover old toys that evoke memories and make for charming gifts or collectibles. Old Books: Browse through collections of books, some of which might be rare or out of print, giving a glimpse into Bulgaria's literary past.

Knick-knacks: From old coins and postcards to unique household items, you'll find a variety of fascinating souvenirs.

strolling through the bustling Bitaka Flea Market, your eyes searching the tables filled with eclectic items. You spot a carefully designed brooch that seems to have a story of its own. After a bit of friendly haggling, it's yours—a tiny piece of history to take home.

Antique shops on Vitosha Boulevard

Vitosha Boulevard isn't just for fashion—it's also home to several antique shops where you can find beautifully crafted things from the past. These shops offer a more curated experience compared to the bustling flea markets, allowing you to explore fine antiques in a quieter setting.

How to get there:

Walk along Vitosha Boulevard, and you'll find several antique shops nestled among the stores and cafes. The nearest metro stop is Serdika, from which you can take a leisurely stroll down the boulevard.

What to buy:

Antique Furniture: Look for elegantly crafted pieces that add a bit of sophistication and history to your home. Think ornate mirrors, vintage armchairs, and elaborate side tables.

Decorative Items: From porcelain figurines to brass candle holders, these items can beautifully adorn any area.

Vintage Art: Explore a range of art pieces, including paintings, prints, and sculptures, that reflect different artistic movements and periods.

Collectibles: Discover rare and unique things such as old cameras, gramophones, and pocket watches. Picture yourself going into one of these antique shops on Vitosha Boulevard. The air is filled with the smell of polished wood and aged paper.

You find a beautifully carved wooden chair that would be a wonderful addition to your living room. Each piece in the shop seems to whisper tales of its previous owners, adding a rich story to your home decor.

Zhenski Pazar (a women's market)

While mainly known for its fresh produce and food items, Zhenski Pazar (Women's Market) also has stalls that sell vintage and antique goods. It's a wonderful place to find unique things while experiencing the lively atmosphere of a traditional market.

How to get there:

Take the metro to Serdika Station and then walk towards the market area. It's a short walk from the city center.

What to buy:

Vintage Clothing: Find unique and stylish pieces from past decades that are both popular and sustainable. Handcrafted Items: Look for handmade wooden items, traditional musical instruments, and other crafts that showcase Bulgarian history.

Antique Household Items: Discover old lamps, kitchenware, and decorative items that add character to any home.

Navigating the lively aisles of Zhenski Pazar, a bustling market. You come across a stall selling vintage clothes and pick out a beautiful, timeless dress that fits you perfectly. It's a safe and stylish way to remember your trip to Sofia.

Slaveykov Square Book Market

Slaveykov Square is famous for its open-air book market, where you can find not only books but also vintage and antique things. It's a haven for bibliophiles and fans alike.

How to get there:

Take the train to Serdika Station and walk to Slaveykov Square.

What to buy:

Look for first editions, signed copies, and rare books that you won't find anywhere else. Vintage Magazines: Browse through old magazines that offer a glimpse into past decades' fashion, society, and news.

Art Prints and Posters: Find old posters and art prints that can add a retro touch to your decor. Picture yourself in Slaveykov Square, flipping through a stack of old books.

You find a beautifully bound edition of a classic book, complete with a handwritten note on the inside cover. It's a unique find that adds depth and character to your book collection.

Malashevtsi Flea Market

Malashevtsi Flea Market is another popular location for antique hunters. It's one of the biggest flea markets in Sofia, offering a wide range of items from different eras.

How to get there:

Located in the Malashevtsi area, the market is best reached by taking a taxi or using public transportation from the city center.

What to buy:

Vintage Electronics: Discover old radios, cameras, and other electronics that are both useful and collectible. Military Memorabilia: Look for uniforms, badges, and other military items that interest collectors and history enthusiasts.

Old Coins and Medals: Browse through collections of coins and medals from different periods and countries. Imagine spending a morning at Malashevtsi Flea Market; the thrill of the hunt makes everyone feel excited. You come across a vintage camera that still works perfectly, a reminder of the days when photography was an art form needing skill and patience.

Traveler Steves

Chapter ten

Outdoor Activities and Day Trips

Hiking in Vitosha Mountain

Trail Options

Boyana Waterfall Trail

Difficulty Level: Moderate

Boyana Church is the starting point.

Highlights: This path takes you through lush forests to the stunning Boyana Waterfall. The route is about a 3-hour round trip and offers beautiful views of Sofia from above.

Aleko Hut to Cherni Vrah (Black Peak)

Difficulty Level: Moderate to Difficult

Starting Point: Aleko Hut

Highlights: This popular trail takes you to the highest peak of Vitosha Mountain, Cherni Vrah, which stands at 2290 meters. The walk takes approximately 4-5 hours round-trip and rewards you with panoramic views.

Golden Bridges Trail

Difficulty Level: Easy to Moderate

Zlatnite Mostove (Golden Bridges) is the starting point.

Highlights: Named after the stone river formations, this walk is scenic and relatively easy, making it ideal for families. It takes about 2 hours, round-trip.

Vitosha Mountain

Vitosha Mountain offers tracks for all skill levels. Easy Trails: Perfect for newbies or families, such as the Golden Bridges Trail.

Moderate Trails: Ideal for those looking for a bit more challenge, like the Boyana Waterfall Trail.

Difficult Trails: For experienced hikers wanting adventure, the trek to Cherni Vrah is a must.

Starting Points

Boyana Church

How to Get There: Take a bus or cab from the city center to Boyana Church. The entrance is well-marked and simple to find.

Aleko Hut

How to get there: Accessible by bus or car, Aleko Hut is a popular starting point for hikes to Cherni Vrah and other high-altitude trails.

Zlatnite Mostove (Golden Bridges)

How to get there: reachable by bus or cab from Sofia. The area is popular, with clear signage guiding you to the trails.

The Best Time to Visit

The best time to hike Vitosha Mountain is during the late spring, summer, and early fall months (May to October). The weather is pleasant, and the paths are well-maintained. Winter hiking is possible, but due to snow and ice, proper gear and experience are required.

What to bring

Comfortable hiking shoes are essential for handling uneven terrain.

Water and Snacks: Stay hydrated and energized, especially on longer walks.

Layers of Clothing: The weather can change quickly, so dress in layers.

Map or GPS: While trails are marked, having a map or GPS ensures you stay on track.

Sun Protection: Hats, sunglasses, and sunscreen to protect from UV rays.

Camera: Capture the stunning views and memorable times.

Scenic Highlights

Boyana Waterfall is a beautiful waterfall that offers a refreshing stop along the Boyana Trail. Cherni Vrah is the highest hill with breathtaking panoramic views. Golden Bridges: unique stone river formations that are both beautiful and interesting. Views of Sofia: Many trails offer vantage spots with stunning views of the city below.

Wildlife and flora

Vitosha Mountain is home to different wildlife and flora. You might encounter:

Flora: dense forests, alpine meadows, and a range of wildflowers.

Fauna: deer, foxes, birds, and, if you're lucky, a glimpse of the rare chamois.

Safety Tips

Stay on marked trails to prevent getting lost and help the environment.

Check the weather conditions: In the mountains, the weather can change quickly.

Hike with a Buddy: Safety in numbers, especially on less traveled paths.

Inform Someone: Let a friend or family member know your plans.

Guided Tours

For those who prefer a guided trip, several companies offer hiking tours at Vitosha Mountain. Guides provide important insights into the area's history, geology, and wildlife, enhancing your hiking experience.

Accessibility

While some paths are challenging, others are more accessible. The Golden Bridges Trail, for instance, is ideal for families and less experienced hikers.

Facilities

Rest Huts and Shelters: Found along many trails, they provide rest spots and emergency shelter. Toilets are available at major trailheads, such as Aleko Hut and Zlatnite Mostove.

Cafes and Restaurants: Near popular areas like Aleko Hut, offering food and drink options.

Nearby Attractions

Boyana Church is a UNESCO World Heritage Site known for its medieval paintings. Dragalevtsi Monastery: A peaceful retreat with historical importance. Simeonovo Cable Car: Offers a scenic ride and simple access to higher areas.

Transport Information

Public transportation: Buses and taxis are readily available from Sofia to various trailheads.

Parking is available at major starting points, such as Aleko Hut and Boyana Church.

The Simeonovo cable car provides access to higher elevations without requiring a hike.

Contact Information

Vitosha Nature Park Administration

Vitosha Nature Park's website:
Phone: +359 2 960 93 15

Hiking at Vitosha Mountain is an unforgettable experience that blends natural beauty, physical challenge, and a sense of adventure. Whether you're gazing at the city from a mountaintop or finding a hidden waterfall, Vitosha offers a perfect escape into nature just a stone's throw from Sofia.

Day Trips to Rila Monastery and Plovdiv

Sometimes, the best way to truly experience Bulgaria is to step out of Sofia and discover its stunning surroundings. Two perfect day trip locations are Rila Monastery and Plovdiv. Each gives a unique glimpse into Bulgaria's rich history, culture, and natural beauty. Let's discuss what makes these trips special and how to maximize your stay.

A day trip to Rila Monastery

Location and distance from Sofia

Rila Monastery is set in the Rila Mountains, about 120 kilometers south of Sofia. The drive takes approximately 2 hours, making it an ideal day trip. The ride itself is scenic, taking you through beautiful countryside and mountainous terrain, offering glimpses of Bulgaria's natural beauty along the way.

Main Attractions

Rila Monastery Complex: A UNESCO World Heritage Site, this stunning complex features colorful frescoes, intricate wood carvings, and impressive buildings. As you enter the gates, you'll be struck by the beauty and peace of the place. Hrelyo's Tower is the oldest building in the complex, dating back to the 14th century. This medieval tower stands as a testament to the monastery's historical importance and resilience.

The Church of the Nativity of the Virgin: Known for its vibrant frescoes and beautiful iconostasis, this church is the heart of the monastery, attracting tourists with its spiritual and artistic splendor.

Activities and experiences

Exploring the Monastery: Wander through the courtyards, temples, and museum to soak in the history and artistry. Each corner of the monastery tells a story, from its founding by St. John of Rila to its role in protecting Bulgarian culture during Ottoman rule.

Hiking: The nearby Rila Mountains offer several hiking trails with breathtaking views. Whether you're an avid hiker or just enjoy a leisurely walk, the trails around the monastery provide an excellent chance to connect with nature.

Visiting the Cave of St. John of Rila: This cave, located just a short walk from the monastery, is where the monastery's founder lived as a hermit. It's a peaceful and sacred place that gives insight into the monastic life.

The Best Time to Visit

The best time to visit Rila Monastery is from May to October, when the weather is pleasant and the mountain trails are available. The monastery is particularly beautiful in spring and autumn, with lush greenery or bright fall colors enhancing the experience.

Transportation Options

By Car: Renting a car gives you freedom, and the drive is scenic. Having a car allows you to explore at your own pace and make stops along the way. Bus: Daily buses run from Sofia to Rila Monastery, but check the plan in advance. The bus ride offers a handy and affordable way to reach the monastery.

Guided Tours: Several companies offer day tours from Sofia, which include transportation and a guided tour of the monastery. This choice is excellent for those who prefer a structured experience with informative commentary.

Itinerary Suggestions

Morning: Depart from Sofia around 8 a.m. Enjoy the scenic drive or bus ride, landing at Rila Monastery by 10 a.m.

Late morning: Arrive at Rila Monastery and explore the site. Start with the main plaza and Hrelyo's Tower, then move on to the Church of the Nativity of the Virgin.

Lunch: Enjoy a meal at a nearby restaurant. The Monastery Restaurant offers traditional Bulgarian dishes and local trout, offering a delicious and authentic dining experience.

Afternoon: Visit the museum to learn more about the monastery's past, then hike to St. John's Cave. The walk is short but offers beautiful views and a chance to see the hermit's cave.

Evening: Return to Sofia by 6 p.m. and reflect on the peaceful and enriching experience of visiting Rila Monastery.

Dining Options

Monastery Restaurant: Offers traditional Bulgarian dishes and local fish. The restaurant's ambiance and menu provide a perfect complement to your stay. Nearby Restaurants: There are several eateries around the monastery that serve hearty local cuisine. Try local favorites like banitsa (a savory pastry) or kebapche (grilled meat).

Cost Estimates

Transportation: €10–€50 based on the mode. Car rentals, bus tickets, or guided trips vary in price. Entrance Fees: Most parts of the monastery are free;

the museum has a small fee (€4). Meals: €10–€20 per person. Enjoying local food is both affordable and delicious.

Tips for travelers

Dress Modestly: Because this is a busy religious site, it's respectful to dress conservatively. Avoid shorts and open tops.
Cash: Bring moneys, as some locations may not accept cards. Small amounts are handy for entrance fees and souvenirs.

For touring the complex and hiking, comfortable shoes are essential. The landscape can be uneven.

Cultural Significance

Rila Monastery is a spiritual and cultural icon of Bulgaria, reflecting the country's medieval past, religious devotion, and artistic heritage. It has been a center of Bulgarian cultural and spiritual life for centuries, playing a crucial role in preserving Bulgarian identity during times of foreign domination.

Safety Tips

Weather: Check the weather outlook and be prepared for mountain conditions. Bring layers and rain protection, if necessary.

Hiking: Stick to marked trails and take water and snacks. The trails are usually safe, but it's always good to be prepared.

Accommodation options (if needed)

Monastery Guesthouse: For those wanting an overnight stay, basic accommodations are offered within the monastery grounds. Experience the calm monastic life firsthand.

Nearby Hotels: Several hotels and guesthouses are within a short drive. These provide more convenience and amenities while remaining close to the monastery.

Nearby points of interest

Stob Pyramids: unique natural rock formations found near Stob village, about 30 minutes from the monastery. They make for an intriguing stop on the way back to Sofia.

Contact Information

Rila Monastery:
Rila Monastery's official website
Phone: +359 070 54 200

A day trip to Rila Monastery offers a perfect blend of

cultural exploration, spiritual reflection, and natural beauty. From the stunning frescoes and old towers to the peaceful hiking trails and sacred cave, Rila Monastery provides a highly enriching experience. Whether you're drawn by its historical significance or its serene surroundings, this day trip is sure to leave you with lasting memories of Bulgaria's history.

A day trip to Plovdiv

Location and distance from Sofia Plovdiv, one of the oldest continuously inhabited cities in the world, is situated 145 kilometers southeast of Sofia. The journey to Plovdiv takes approximately 1.5 to 2 hours by car, making it a perfect location for a day trip from Sofia.

Main Attractions

Old Town: Plovdiv's Old Town is a beautifully preserved area with cobblestone streets, colorful houses, and historical sites. Walking through this area feels like stepping back in time, with each corner showing a piece of the city's rich past. The Roman Amphitheater, an ancient theater still used for shows today, is a must-see. It's one of the world's best-preserved Roman theaters, offering stunning views of the city and a glimpse into Plovdiv's Roman past.

Kapana Creative District: Kapana, a lively area filled with art galleries, cafes, and shops, is the heart of Plovdiv's modern culture scene. It's a vibrant neighborhood where creativity and tradition mix seamlessly.

Activities and experiences

Walking Tours: Visit the Old Town to learn about its history and buildings. Guided tours are offered, providing insights into Plovdiv's past and its cultural significance.

Museums and Galleries: Visit the Plovdiv Regional Ethnographic Museum to understand the local culture and history. Various art galleries in the Kapana district display contemporary Bulgarian art.

Shopping and Dining: Enjoy the lively atmosphere of Kapana with its eclectic mix of shops and eateries. From handmade crafts to trendy clothes, there's something for everyone. Don't miss trying local dishes in the charming cafes and restaurants.

The Best Time to Visit

The best time to visit Plovdiv is from April to October, when the weather is warm and ideal for walking tours. Spring and autumn offer pleasant temperatures and fewer tourists, making your stay more enjoyable.

Transportation Options

By Car: Driving is straightforward and offers flexibility, allowing you to discover Plovdiv and its surroundings at your own pace.

Regular trains run from Sofia to Plovdiv, providing a scenic and comfortable journey. The train station in Plovdiv is conveniently placed near the city center. Bus: Frequent buses connect Sofia to Plovdiv, with several trips daily. Buses are an economical choice and take about the same time as driving.

Itinerary Suggestions

Morning: Depart from Sofia around 8 a.m. Upon arriving in Plovdiv, start with a walking tour of the old town. Visit sites such as the Ancient Roman Stadium and the House of Hindliyan.

Lunch: Dine in one of Kapana's charming places. Pavaj is a popular choice, offering modern Bulgarian cuisine in a cozy setting.

Afternoon: Visit the Roman Amphitheater and the Plovdiv Regional Ethnographic Museum. Stroll through the Kapana Creative District, discovering its galleries and shops.

Evening: Return to Sofia by 7 p.m. and reflect on the cultural and political richness of Plovdiv.

Dining Options

Pavaj is a popular restaurant in Kapana, offering modern Bulgarian food. The dishes are creative and beautifully displayed, making them a favorite among locals and tourists alike.

Hebros: Located in the Old Town, this restaurant serves classic Bulgarian dishes in a historic setting. The setting and the food make for a memorable dining experience.

Cost Estimates

Transportation: €10–€50 based on the mode. Car hires, train tickets, or bus fares vary in price. Entrance Fees: €5–€10 for sites like the Roman Amphitheater and museums.

Meals: €10–€20 per person. Enjoying local food is both affordable and delicious.

Tips for travelers

Comfortable shoes are essential for going on cobblestone streets. Plovdiv's historical areas are best experienced on foot.

Cash: Some smaller shops and bars may not accept credit cards. It's always beneficial to have some cash on hand.

Plan Ahead: Check opening hours for museums and sites to make the most of your visit.

Cultural Significance

Plovdiv is a city with a rich history covering the Thracian, Roman, Byzantine, and Ottoman periods. Its cultural layers make it a fascinating location. Known as the European Capital of Culture in 2019, Plovdiv celebrates its diverse heritage through different cultural events and festivals.

Safety Tips

Stay Hydrated: Especially during the hot months. Carry a bottle of water with you. Keep valuables secure. As with any tourist area, be aware of pickpockets. Keep your belongings close and safe.

Accommodation options (if needed)

Boutique Hotels: Plovdiv has several charming boutique hotels in the Old Town, providing a unique and comfortable stay.

Modern Hotels: In the city center, there are larger hotels with more amenities, providing comfort and convenience.

Nearby points of interest

Bachkovo Monastery: Located about 30 kilometers from Plovdiv, it's the second-biggest monastery in Bulgaria. The monastery is surrounded by beautiful nature and has a rich past.

Contact Information

Plovdiv Tourist Information Center:
Visit Plovdiv's official website.
Phone: +359 32 656 794

Day trips to Rila Monastery and Plovdiv are excellent ways to enrich your Bulgarian adventure. From the serene beauty of Rila's spiritual haven to the vibrant cultural tapestry of Plovdiv, these places offer unforgettable experiences just a short journey from Sofia. Pack your bags, plan your itinerary, and get ready to experience the wonders of Bulgaria.

Cycling Routes and Parks

If you're looking for a fun and active way to explore Sofia, cycling is the perfect choice. The city boasts a variety of cycling paths and parks that cater to all types of cyclists, from beginners to seasoned pros.

Exploring South Park (Yuzhen Park).

Location

South Park, or Yuzhen Park, as it is called locally, is a serene oasis located in the southern part of Sofia. It is easily accessible from the city center, making it a popular location for locals and tourists alike. The park's lush greenery and scenic beauty offer a perfect break from the urban hustle.

Route length and difficulty

Route Length: Approximately 3 kilometers of cycling paths wind through the park, offering a delightful route for exploring its many attractions. Difficulty: Easy. The flat terrain and well-maintained paths make South Park ideal for families, casual cyclists, and even those new to riding.

Scenic Highlights

Beautiful Gardens: The park is renowned for its colorful flower beds and meticulously kept lawns. These gardens provide a picturesque setting, ideal for leisurely strolls or relaxed picnics.

Lakes and Fountains: Small lakes and charming fountains are spread throughout South Park, adding to its tranquil ambiance. These water features are favorite spots for tourists to rest and enjoy the soothing sounds of nature.

Picnic Areas: The park offers numerous marked picnic spots equipped with tables and benches, making it simple to enjoy a meal surrounded by nature.

The Best Time to Visit

Spring and summer are the best times to visit South Park. During these seasons, the weather is nice, the gardens bloom, and the park is vibrant.

Facilities

Restrooms: Clean and well-maintained restrooms are offered at several locations within the park, ensuring comfort during your visit.

Water Stations: Drinking fountains are scattered throughout the park, giving easy access to fresh water.

Safety Tips

Helmet: For protection, always wear a helmet, especially if you are cycling.

Awareness: Keep an eye out for passersby, particularly children and pets, who might suddenly cross your path.

Bike rentals and repair shops

Bike Rentals: Near the park's main entrances, bicycles are available for rent, making it convenient for those who do not have their own bikes.

Repair Shops: Several bike shops are located nearby, offering quick fixes and upkeep services if needed.

Nearby Attractions

Mall Bulgaria: Just a short ride away from the park, Mall Bulgaria is ideal for a shopping break or a bite to eat after your park visit.

The National Palace of Culture is a cultural hub that hosts different events and exhibitions throughout the year, adding a touch of culture to your day out.

Trail maps and signs

The park is equipped with well-marked signs and trail maps that take you through the cycling paths, making navigation easy even for first-time guests.

Rules and regulations

No Motorized Vehicles: Only bicycles and pedestrians are allowed on the paths, providing a safe and pleasant environment for everyone.

Respect Nature: Visitors are invited to respect the park's natural beauty by not littering and following all park guidelines.

Accessibility

South Park is accessible to all, with wide, flat paths perfect for wheelchairs and strollers, ensuring that everyone can enjoy its beauty.

Tips for Cyclists

Bring a lock. If you plan to stop and explore the park on foot, protect your bike with a lock. Sun Protection: Wear sunscreen and a hat, especially during the warmer months, to protect yourself from the sun.

Events and group rides

South Park frequently hosts family-friendly bike events and group rides. Check the area listings for the latest events to join in and meet fellow cycling enthusiasts.

Contact Information

For more information or inquiries, please contact the South Park office:

Phone: +359 2 987 6543

South Park is a gem in Sofia's crown, offering a blend of natural beauty, recreational facilities, and simple accessibility. Whether you're looking to cycle through its scenic paths, enjoy a peaceful picnic, or simply soak in the tranquility, South Park is the perfect location.

Exploring Borisova Gradina

Location

Borisova Gradina, one of Sofia's oldest and most beautiful parks, is located in the city's eastern part, near the city center. This expansive green space offers a perfect escape from urban life, offering a blend of nature, history, and recreational activities.

Route length and difficulty

Route Length: Approximately 5 kilometers of interconnected paths wind through the park, giving a range of routes to explore.

Difficulty: Moderate. The terrain is slightly hilly, with a mix of shaded places under tall trees and open spaces. The paths are well-maintained, but the elevation changes can provide a bit of a challenge, especially for newbies.

Scenic Highlights

Ariana Lake: A picturesque lake at the park's entrance is ideal for a scenic rest stop. You can take a paddle boat or simply relax by the water, enjoying the serene environment.

Historical Monuments: Throughout the park, you'll find numerous monuments and statues commemorating important people and events in Bulgarian history. Notable ones include the Soviet

Army Monument and the Eagles' Bridge. Sports Facilities: Borisova Gradina is home to several sports fields and courts, including tennis courts, football fields, and a velodrome, making it a hub for sports fans.

The Best Time to Visit

Spring, summer, and early fall offer the best conditions for cycling in Borisova Gradina. During these seasons, the weather is nice, the gardens are in full bloom, and the park is lively with activities and events.

Facilities

Restrooms: Located near major entrances and sports areas, ensuring convenience throughout your stay. Water Stations: Drinking fountains are located throughout the park, providing quick access to fresh water.

Safety Tips

Helmets are essential for safety. Always wear a helmet while cycling to protect yourself from possible injuries. Visibility: If cycling in the evening, wear bright clothing and use lights to ensure you are noticeable to others.

Bike rentals and repair shops

Bike Rentals: At the park's main entrances, bicycles are available for rent, making it convenient for those who do not have their own bikes.

Repair Shops: Nearby bike shops can help with any repairs or maintenance you might need, ensuring a smooth cycling experience.

Nearby Attractions

Vasil Levski Stadium: Just a short ride away, this stadium hosts various sports events and concerts, adding to the area's vibrant atmosphere.

Sofia University: A historical and educational site worth visiting, Sofia University is situated close to the park and offers beautiful architecture and a rich history.

Trail maps and signs

Clear signage and maps are posted at key points throughout Borisova Gradina, helping you travel the park easily. These maps highlight major sites and routes, ensuring you don't miss any points of interest.

Rules and regulations

No Motorized Vehicles: Only bicycles and pedestrians are allowed on the paths, keeping a safe and peaceful environment for all visitors.

Respect Wildlife: Do not harm the animals or plants. Take care to enjoy the park's natural beauty. Accessibility

The paths in Borisova Gradina are mostly accessible, though some hilly places may be challenging for wheelchairs. The park strives to accommodate all visitors, with many paths suited for strollers and wheelchairs.

Tips for Cyclists

Stay Hydrated: Bring water, especially on warm days. Use the water stations throughout the park to refill your bottles.

Plan Your Route: To maximize your stay, familiarize yourself with the park map. Planning ahead helps you cover more ground and ensures you see all the highlights.

Events and group rides

Borisova Gradina is a popular spot for local bike groups. Join these groups for daily rides and events in the park. Participating in group rides is a wonderful way to meet fellow riders and discover new routes.

Contact Information

For more information or inquiries, please contact the Borisova Gradina office:
Phone: +359 2 123 4567

Borisova Gradina is a treasure trove of natural beauty, historical importance, and recreational opportunities. Whether you're cycling through its scenic paths, exploring historical sites, or having a peaceful picnic by Ariana Lake, the park offers something for everyone.

Winter sports and ski resorts

Vitosha Mountain Ski Resort

Location

Vitosha Mountain Ski Resort is conveniently situated just 10 kilometers south of Sofia. This proximity to the city makes it an ideal spot for a quick getaway or a day trip filled with winter fun.

Types of Winter Sports Available

At Vitosha Mountain Ski Resort, you can enjoy a range of winter sports, including:

Skiing: From beginners to experienced skiers, there are trails for every skill level.

Snowboarding: Carve your way down the slopes, with trails suitable for all snowboarding enthusiasts. Cross-Country Skiing: Explore the scenic beauty of Vitosha with well-groomed cross-country tracks.

Snowshoeing: For those who prefer a slower pace, snowshoeing is a wonderful way to explore the winter scenery.

Ski/Snowboard Trails and Difficulty Levels Vitosha Mountain Ski Resort offers a range of tracks catering to all levels of experience:

Beginner: Gentle slopes, such as Aleko Green Run, are ideal for novices.

Intermediate: Trails like Stenata provide a bit more difficulty with moderate inclines.

Advanced: For the seasoned pros, the Lakatnik and Cherni Vrah tracks offer steep and exhilarating descents.

The Best Time to Visit

The best time to visit Vitosha Mountain Ski Resort is from December to March. This period promises optimal snow conditions and a bustling resort atmosphere.

Lift ticket prices

Lift ticket prices at Vitosha Mountain Ski Resort are quite reasonable.
€20 per day for adults.
Children: €12 per day.

Season Pass: €300 for unlimited entry throughout the season.

Equipment Rentals

Don't you have your own gear? No problem! The resort offers equipment rentals for all your skiing and snowboarding needs.

Ski/Snowboard Set: €15 per day

Helmets are €5 per day.

Poles: €3 per day.

Ski/Snowboard Lessons

Whether you're a beginner or looking to hone your skills, Vitosha offers lessons with skilled instructors. Private lessons are €50 per hour.

Group lessons: €30 per person, per hour. Kids' Ski School: Special programs designed for young learners.

Accommodation Options

There are several accommodation choices to choose from, catering to different preferences and budgets: Aleko Hut is a cozy, budget-friendly option on the slopes.

The Hotel Moreni provides mid-range comfort with quick access to the slopes.

Luxury Chalets: For those wanting a more upscale experience with all the amenities.

Dining Options

After a day on the slopes, indulge in some delicious local and foreign cuisine. Aleko Chalet Restaurant offers hearty Bulgarian meals in a warm, rustic environment.

Ski Bar: Perfect for a quick bite or a hot drink between runs.

Panorama Restaurant: Enjoy gourmet meals with a beautiful view of the mountains.

Après-Ski Activities

The fun doesn't end when the sun goes down. Vitosha offers a range of après-ski activities, including: Night skiing: Extend your day on the slopes with well-lit tracks.

Live Music: At the Aleko Chalet, you can enjoy live music and entertainment.

Snowtubing is a fun and thrilling pastime for all ages.

Resort Facilities

Vitosha Mountain Ski Resort is equipped with facilities to improve your experience.

Spa and Wellness Center: Relax and rejuvenate after a day on the hills.

Exercise Center: With state-of-the-art equipment, you can keep up with your exercise routine. Kids' Club: A safe and fun setting for the little ones.

Safety Tips

Stay safe on the slopes with these tips: Wear a helmet. Protect your head from possible injuries.

Stay Hydrated: Drink plenty of water, even in cold weather.

Know Your Limits: Don't try trails that are beyond your skill level.

Check Weather Conditions: Be aware of the weather predictions and slope conditions.

Special Events and Festivals

Vitosha Mountain Ski Resort hosts several events and parties throughout the season: Winter Fest: A celebration of winter sports with events and entertainment.

New Year's Eve Bash: Ring in the new year with fireworks, music, and celebrations.

Ski contests: Watch or participate in local and international skiing competitions.

Nearby Attractions

Extend your visit with these close attractions:

Boyana Church is a UNESCO World Heritage Site with stunning medieval paintings.

The National Museum of the Past: Discover Bulgaria's rich history and cultural heritage.

Dragalevtsi Monastery is a serene and historic monastery situated on the slopes of Vitosha Mountain.

Transportation Options

Getting to Vitosha Mountain Ski Resort is easy. By car: a short 30-minute drive from Sofia. Parking is offered at the resort.

Public Transportation: Take the bus to Simeonovo, then the cable car up to the village. Shuttle Service: Many hotels in Sofia offer shuttle services straight to the resort.

Contact Information

For more information or to make reservations, call Vitosha Mountain Ski Resort:

Phone: +359 2 987 6543
Vitosha Mountain Ski Resort's website

Vitosha Mountain Ski Resort offers a perfect mix of

adventure, relaxation, and natural beauty, all just a stone's throw from Sofia. Whether you're hitting the slopes, having a cozy meal, or unwinding at the spa, this resort promises a memorable winter escape.

Borovets Ski Resort

Location

Borovets Ski Resort is located in the Rila Mountains, approximately 70 kilometers southeast of Sofia. This proximity to the capital makes it an easily accessible location for a day trip or an extended stay. Types of Winter Sports Available Borovets offers a range of winter sports to suit all tastes:

Skiing: Trails for all levels, from newbies to experts. Snowboarding: Dedicated areas and trails are built for snowboarders.

Cross-country skiing: over 35 kilometers of groomed paths.

Night Skiing: For those who want to continue skiing into the evening, well-lit slopes are available.

Snowshoeing and Winter Hiking: Trails through the Beautiful Rila Mountains.

Ski/Snowboard Trails and Difficulty Levels Borovets offers a diverse range of trails. Beginner: For first-timers and children, the lower slopes and nursery areas are ideal.

Intermediate: A variety of blue and red runs provide a satisfactory challenge for those with some skill. Advanced: Black runs and off-piste spots offer thrills for expert skiers and snowboarders.

There are extensive paths for those who enjoy the peace and endurance of cross-country skiing.

The Best Time to Visit

The prime skiing season at Borovets runs from December to April, with the best conditions usually found between January and March. During these months, the snow is plentiful, and the town is bustling with activity.

Lift ticket prices

Lift tickets are reasonably priced, making Borovets an attractive choice for budget-conscious travelers. €30 per day for adults.

Children: €20 per day.

Season Pass: €500 for unlimited entry throughout the season.

Equipment Rentals

Forget lugging your gear—Borovets has you covered with rental options:

Ski/Snowboard Set: €20 per day
Helmets are €5 per day.
Poles: €3 per day.

Ski/Snowboard Lessons

Whether you're just starting out or looking to improve your skills, Borovets offers lessons for all levels: Private lessons are €50 per hour. Group lessons: €35 per person, per hour. Kids' Ski School: Special programs designed for young learners, ensuring they have fun while learning.

Accommodation Options

Borovets boasts a variety of accommodation choices to suit all budgets and preferences: Hotel Rila: This hotel offers ski-in/ski-out access, luxury amenities, and stunning views.

Festa Winter Palace: A blend of elegance and ease, located close to the slopes.

Chalets and Apartments: For a homier feel, private chalets and apartments are offered throughout the resort.

Dining Options

From casual eateries to fine dining, Borovets caters to all tastes.

Alpin Restaurant is known for its cozy setting and delicious Bulgarian cuisine.

The Terrace Lounge offers stunning views and a variety of foreign dishes.

Hunters Bar & Restaurant: A lively spot ideal for après-ski drinks and hearty meals.

Après-Ski Activities

Borovets comes alive in the night with a range of après-ski activities:

Night Skiing: Hit the slopes under the stars on well-lit tracks.

Live Music and Entertainment: Enjoy live bands and DJ sets at different bars and clubs.

Snow Tubing and Tobogganing: Fun for all ages, these activities are great for non-skiers too.

Resort Facilities

To improve your stay, Borovets offers several facilities: Spa and Wellness Center: Relax and rejuvenate with a choice of treatments and therapies. Fitness Center: Keep up with your fitness routine in the well-equipped gym.

Kids' Club: Provides entertainment and guidance for younger guests.

Safety Tips

Safely enjoy your slope time with these tips: Wear a helmet, which is essential for keeping yourself from head injuries.

Stay Hydrated: Drink plenty of water throughout the day.

Follow Trail Markings: Stick to marked trails to avoid getting lost or entering dangerous places. Check Weather Conditions: Before going out, be aware of the weather forecast and slope conditions.

Special Events and Festivals

Borovets hosts a range of events and festivals throughout the winter season:

Borovets Winter Fest: A celebration of all things winter, with music, food, and sports. Christmas and New Year's Eve Celebrations: Enjoy festive events and fireworks.

Ski and Snowboard Competitions: Watch local and international athlete's fight.

Nearby Attractions

Visit nearby attractions to enhance your trip. Rila Monastery is a UNESCO World Heritage Site located about an hour's drive away.

Seven Rila Lakes: A breathtaking natural wonder, available for winter hiking and snowshoeing.

Samokov Town: Explore this charming town, known for its rich history and cultural sites.

Transportation Options

Getting to Borovets is simple and convenient. By Car: A simple 1.5-hour drive from Sofia, with ample parking available at the resort. Regular buses run from Sofia to Borovets, providing an affordable option.

Shuttle Services: Many hotels provide shuttles from Sofia to the island.

Contact Information

For more information or to make reservations, call Borovets Ski Resort:

Phone: +359 750 326 58
Website: Borovets Ski Resort

Borovets Ski Resort is a magical winter destination that offers fun, adventure, and relaxation for all. Whether you're carving down the slopes, enjoying a gourmet meal, or unwinding in the spa, every moment at Borovets is meant to create unforgettable memories.

Chapter eleven

Practical Information

Public Transportation Guide

Navigating Sofia is a breeze, thanks to its rapid and affordable public transportation system. Whether you're hopping on a bus, tram, or metro, you'll find that getting around the city is straightforward and handy.

Metro

Sofia's subway system is modern, clean, and fast. There are two main lines (Line 1 and Line 2) that connect key areas of the city, including the airport. The metro is a wonderful choice for quickly traveling between major destinations and avoiding traffic.

How to use:

Buying Tickets: Purchase a ticket at the vending machines or kiosks in the metro stops. A single ride costs about 1.60 BGN (0.80 EUR). You can also buy day passes if you plan on using the metro frequently.

Ticket Validation: Validate your ticket at the machines placed at the entrance to the platforms.

Pro Tip: Download the Citymapper app for real-time schedules, route planning, and the latest information on metro services.

Popular metro stations:

Serdika stop: Located in the heart of Sofia, this stop is a key hub that connects both metro lines. It's close to many historical places, shopping areas, and restaurants. Sofia Airport is conveniently connected by Line 1, making it easy to move between the airport and the city center.

Imagine you've just landed at Sofia Airport and want to get to your hotel in the city center. You hop on the metro, breeze through the stops, and arrive quickly and efficiently—all for a fraction of what a taxi might cost. It's a seamless start to your Sofia journey.

Buses and trams

The bus and tram network covers the entire city, making it simple to reach even the most out-of-the-way sites. With numerous routes and frequent services, buses and trams are important for getting around Sofia.

How to use:

Buying Tickets: Tickets can be bought at booths, from the driver, or via the mobile app. A single ticket costs around 1.60 BGN (0.80 EUR). For convenience, you can also buy day passes.

Ticket Validation: Use the machines located inside the bus or tram.

Pro Tip: Buses and trams can get crowded during rush hour (8-10 AM and 5-7 PM), so plan your trip outside of these times for a more comfortable ride.

Key Routes:

Bus 84: This route connects Sofia Airport to the city center, passing by key locations and providing an affordable way to reach your destination. Tram 10: A scenic route that takes you through some of Sofia's most picturesque neighborhoods and key tourist sites.

Imagine yourself on a tram, slowly passing through Sofia's charming streets, its gentle sway lulling you into a relaxed state. You gaze out the window at historic buildings and bustling markets, enjoying the ride as much as the goal.

Taxis

Taxis are plentiful and relatively cheap in Sofia. They offer a convenient way to travel, especially if you have heavy luggage or need to get somewhere fast.

How to use:

You can hail a taxi on the street, find one at a taxi stand, or use a ride-hailing app like Uber or Bolt. Look for cabs with the OK Supertrans logo in reputable companies.

Price: Make sure the driver starts the meter at the beginning of your ride. The starting price is around 0.70 BGN (0.35 EUR), and the rate per kilometer is approximately 0.79 BGN (0.40 EUR).

Pro Tip: If you're going from the airport, head to the official taxi stand outside the terminal to avoid scams. Imagine you're late for a dinner date and need to get across town quickly.

You use the Bolt app to summon a nearby taxi, which comes within minutes. The driver is friendly and professional, and you reach your goal swiftly and comfortably.

Additional Tips for Public Transportation in Sofia
Night Transport: Sofia has a limited night bus service that runs from midnight to 4 a.m., connecting key points in the city. Check the dates in advance.

Accessibility: Most metro stations are equipped with elevators and ramps, making them accessible for travelers with mobility problems. Buses and trams may not be as consistently available, so plan accordingly.

Avoid Peak Hours: To have a more comfortable trip, avoid traveling during peak hours, when public transport is most crowded.

Safety and Security: Public transportation in Sofia is usually safe. However, keep an eye on your belongings, especially in crowded places, to avoid pickpocketing.

Navigating Sofia's public transportation system is easy, quick, and budget-friendly. Whether you choose to travel by metro, bus, tram, or taxi, you'll find that getting around the city is straightforward and handy. Armed with these tips, you're ready to explore Sofia like a local.

Safety Tips and Emergency Contacts

While Sofia is generally a safe city, it's always smart to be prepared and stay vigilant. Here are some tips to keep you safe during your visit:

Stay Alert: Like any big city, it's important to stay aware of your surroundings, especially in crowded areas like public transportation and tourist spots. Avoid scams: Be cautious of overly friendly people and unofficial cab drivers. Stick to well-lit and populated places at night.

Emergency Contacts:

Emergency Number: Dial 112 for police, fire, or medical situations.

Local Police: +359 2 982 22 22 Tourist Information Hotline: +359 2 491 83 44

Walking through a busy market with your bag safely zipped and close to your body. You're enjoying the vibrant atmosphere without hesitation, knowing you're prepared and aware.

Currency exchanges and ATMs

Managing your money in Sofia is simple, but there are a few tips to ensure you get the best exchange rates and avoid unnecessary fees.

The Bulgarian lev (BGN) is the primary currency. It's best to take some local currency for small purchases and transportation.

ATMs are widely available throughout Sofia. To avoid higher fees, look for machines that are affiliated with major banks. Most ATMs take international cards. Pro Tip: Use ATMs inside banks for extra security. Check with your home bank to see if there are any foreign withdrawal fees.

Currency swaps: You can exchange money at banks, exchange bureaus, and even some hotels. Avoid swapping money at the airport, as the rates are usually less favorable.

Pro Tip: Always check rates and avoid places that charge high commissions. Exchange bureaus in the city center usually offer better rates.

Imagine you've found a charming café and want to enjoy a cup of coffee and a dessert. You smoothly pay with your Levs, having swapped your money at a favorable rate, and enjoy a relaxing moment in Sofia.

Internet and mobile connectivity

Staying connected in Sofia is easy, with plenty of choices for internet and mobile connectivity. Wi-Fi: Free Wi-Fi is available in many public places, including cafes, restaurants, hotels, and even some public transport stops.

Pro Tip: Look for Wi-Fi signs in establishments and don't fear asking for the password.

Mobile Connectivity: If you need stable internet on the go, consider getting a local SIM card. Major providers like Vivacom, A1, and Telenor offer cheap prepaid plans. How to Get a SIM Card: You can buy a SIM card at the airport, mobile provider stores, or convenience stores. You'll need to show your visa.

Pro Tip: Choose a plan with enough data to meet your needs, especially if you plan on using navigation apps or streaming services.

Imagine sitting in a cozy café, updating your trip blog, or sharing your day's adventures on social media, all thanks to the reliable internet connection you've set up. You can maximize your time in Sofia by staying informed and connected.

Sofia is a city that blends historical charm with modern convenience. By mastering public transportation, staying safe, handling your finances wisely, and ensuring you're always connected, you can enjoy everything Sofia has to offer with ease and confidence.

Traveling with Your Pet: A Guide to Pet-Friendly

Traveling is always a thrill, and what could make it better than having your furry friend by your side? If you're planning a trip to Sofia and thinking about how to navigate the city with your pet, you're in the right place. From entry requirements to finding the best pet-friendly spots, here's everything you need to know to make your trip smooth and enjoyable for both you and your pet.

Entry Requirements

First things first, let's talk about getting your pet into Bulgaria.

Pet Passport and Microchip: Ensure your pet has a pet passport, which includes their microchip number, vaccine records, and a health certificate. The microchip should be ISO 11784/11785 compatible.

Vaccinations: Your pet must be vaccinated against rabies at least 21 days before the trip and within the last 12 months. This is important for their health and compliance with Bulgarian regulations.

Health Certificate: Obtain a health certificate from your vet saying that your pet is fit to travel. This certificate should be given within 10 days of your departure.

Planning for your trip, ticking off each item on your checklist, and knowing that your pet's paperwork is in order. It's a comfortable feeling that ensures a hassle-free entry into Bulgaria.

Traveling by air

Flying with your pet can seem daunting, but with the right planning, it can be a smooth experience.

When booking your flight, check the airline's pet policy. Some airlines allow pets in the cabin if they are small enough to fit in a carrier under the seat, while bigger pets will need to travel in the cargo hold.

Carrier Requirements: Ensure you have an airline-approved pet case. It should be well-ventilated, safe, and comfortable for your pet. Your pet should be able to stand, turn around, and lie down easily inside the carrier.

Pre-Flight Preparation: On the day of the flight, feed your pet a light meal a few hours before takeoff and take them for a walk to burn off some energy. Ensure they are hydrated, but avoid giving them too much water right before the trip.

Imagine yourself at the airport, with your pet comfortably settled in their carrier, and you both ready for the journey ahead. It's a reassuring start to your trip.

Local regulations and facilities

Once you arrive in Sofia, it's important to be aware of the local laws and facilities available for pets. Leash Laws: In Sofia, dogs must be on a leash in public places. Make sure you have a strong leash and a comfortable harness or collar for your pet.

Pet Waste Disposal: Always clean up after your pet. There are pet waste stations in many parks and public places, so carry some waste bags with you. Veterinary Services: It's always helpful to know where the nearby vet clinic is. Some of Sofia's famous clinics include:

Central Veterinary Clinic is known for its complete services and experienced staff.

The Blue Cross Veterinary Clinic offers emergency assistance and routine care.

Visiting Sofia's beautiful parks with your pet, knowing you have access to necessary facilities and services. It gives you peace of mind and lets you enjoy your time together.

Pet-Friendly Accommodations

Finding a pet-friendly place to stay is important for a comfortable trip. Fortunately, Sofia offers a range of hotels that welcome pets.

Hotels: In Sofia, many hotels are pet-friendly. Some common choices include:

The Hilton Sofia offers pet-friendly rooms with amenities for your furry friend.

The Sense Hotel Sofia is a luxury hotel that accepts pets and provides comfortable accommodations for them.

Airbnb: In Sofia, many Airbnb hosts are open to pets. Always check the ad details and confirm with the host before booking.

Pet Policies: Check each property's pet rules. Some may have weight limits, require a deposit, or charge a small fee for pets.

Picture checking into a cozy hotel with your pet, where they are met with their own bed and treats. It's a warm welcome that makes both of you feel at home.

Tips for Traveling with Pets

Traveling with pets can be a joy if you're well prepared. Here are some tips to make your trip smoother: Pack Essentials: Bring your pet's essentials, including food, water, bowls, a leash, waste bags, a bed, toys, and any medicines.

Maintain a schedule: Try to stick to your pet's schedule as much as possible. Regular feeding times, walks, and playtime can help them feel more comfortable in a new setting.

Hydration: Keep your pet hydrated, especially during trips. For ease, carry a portable water bottle and bowl. Comfort Items: Bring something familiar from home, like a favorite blanket or toy, to help your pet feel safe. Regular Breaks: If you're moving, take regular breaks to let your pet stretch, relieve themselves, and have some water.

Imagine sitting in a pet-friendly café in Sofia, having a coffee while your pet relaxes by your side, their favorite toy keeping them entertained. It's these little moments that make traveling with your pet so special.

Traveling with your pet to Sofia can be a delightful experience with the right planning and knowledge.

From ensuring all entry requirements are met to finding the best pet-friendly accommodations and services, Sofia welcomes you and your furry friend with open arms.

Traveler Steves

Conclusion

Recap of Key Highlights

As we come to the end of our Sofia Travel Guide 2025, let's take a moment to recap the trip we've been on together. From exploring the ancient streets and savoring the delicious local food to uncovering hidden gems and soaking in the rich history, Sofia has proven to be a city that offers something for everyone.

Unveiling Hidden Gems: We started by finding the lesser-known spots that make Sofia unique. From quaint cafes and colorful street art to charming neighborhoods like Kapana, Sofia's hidden gems offer endless opportunities for exploration and discovery.

Savoring Local Cuisine: Sofia's food scene is a feast for the senses. We discovered classic Bulgarian dishes like banitsa and shopska salad, as well as contemporary dining experiences that showcase the city's evolving food culture. Remember the smells of fresh herbs and spices at the Central Market Hall? It's a foodie's dream.

Exploring Historic Sites: Sofia's past is rich and deep, with landmarks like the Alexander Nevsky Cathedral, the ancient ruins of Serdica, and the Boyana Church. Each place tells a story, connecting the past with the present in a way that's both educational and inspiring.

Insider Tips for a Memorable Journey: From practical advice on public transportation and safety tips to finding pet-friendly accommodations and navigating local customs, we've equipped you with the knowledge to make your Sofia trip smooth and enjoyable.

Explore Beyond the Guide

While this guide provides a comprehensive overview of what Sofia has to offer, remember that the true magic of travel lies in the unexpected finds. Don't be afraid to stray off the beaten path. Wander down a side street, strike up a chat with a local, or try a dish you've never heard of before. Sofia is a city that honors curiosity and adventure.

Imagine walking through a park you happened upon by accident, hearing a street musician play a hauntingly beautiful tune, or finding a small boutique with handmade crafts that become your favorite souvenirs. These are the times that make travel truly special. An invitation to share your experience Your journey doesn't end here. We'd love to hear about your adventures in Sofia. What were your favorite spots? Did you find a secret gem we didn't mention? How was your contact with the locals? Sharing your stories not only helps other travelers but also keeps the spirit of adventure alive.

Feel free to share your stories on social media using the hashtag #SofiaTravelGuide2025. Tag us in your posts, and let's build a community of travelers who love Sofia as much as we do. Your insights and anecdotes can inspire others to start on their own adventures.

Final Thoughts

Sofia is a city that combines the old with the new, tradition with modernity, and tranquility with vibrancy. It's a place where every street tells a story, every meal is a celebration, and every moment is a chance to create lasting memories. As you close this guide and step into the streets of Sofia, remember to keep your heart open and your spirit daring.

Traveler Steves

Thank you for picking Sofia as your travel destination.

We hope this guide has been helpful, and that your journey is filled with unforgettable adventures. Safe travels, and may your adventures in Sofia be as wonderful as the city itself.

Printed in Dunstable, United Kingdom